http://design.coda.drexel.edu/Faculty/
johnlangdon/wordplay.html

JOHN LANGDON

AMBIGRAMS
AND

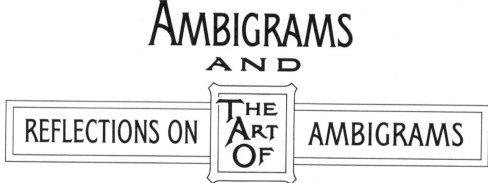

REFLECTIONS ON THE ART OF AMBIGRAMS

Harcourt Brace Jovanovich, Publishers
New York   San Diego   London

Requests for permission to make copies of any part
of the work should be mailed to: Permissions Department,
Harcourt Brace Jovanovich, Publishers, 8th floor,
Orlando, Florida 32887.

The lyrics to the Byrds' recording "Turn! Turn! Turn! (To Everything There Is a Season)"
are used with the permission of Melody Trails and The Richmond Organization. The words
were adapted from the Book of Ecclesiastes by Pete Seeger. TRO—© Copyright 1962 (renewed)
Melody Trails, Inc., New York, NY. Material from J. Bronowski's *Science and Human Values*
is quoted with the permission of Simon & Schuster; material from Paul Williams's *Das Energi*,
with the permission of Warner Books; material from Alan Watts's *Tao: The Watercourse Way*,
with the permission of Pantheon Books; three lines from T. S. Eliot's *Four Quartets* with the
permission of Harcourt Brace Jovanovich. Escher's *Circle Limit IV*, *Sky and Water I*, *Relativity*,
and *Waterfall* (all Collection Haags Geurecrite Museum, the Hague) are reproduced with the
permission of Cordon Art B.V., Holland.

Library of Congress Cataloging-in-Publication Data
Langdon, John, 1946–
Wordplay: ambigrams & reflections
on the art of ambigrams/John Langdon.—1st ed.
p.   cm.
Includes bibliographical references.
ISBN 0-15-198454-9
1. Calligraphy.   2. Play on words.   3. Ambiguity.   I. Title.
Z43.L259   1992
745.6′1—dc20   91-36095

Designed by Trina Stahl and John Langdon
Printed in the United States of America
First edition
A B C D E

To my family—past, present, and future

CONTENTS

vii

ACKNOWLEDGMENTS

I OWE A DEBT of gratitude to a number of people who contributed to this book, both visibly and invisibly.

Douglas Hofstadter introduced me to my editor, Anne Freedgood, whose belief in ambigrams and *Wordplay* has made a fantasy into a reality. Anne put me in touch with Christopher Bouchard, whose broad knowledge of widely disparate subjects from Taoism to history, literature and science helped establish a direction for the essays at the outset. After the writing was complete, his expertise in physics saved me from more than a couple of embarrassing mistakes.

David Slavitt's enthusiastic encouragement gave

me the confidence to leap headlong into the writing. In addition, David provided a jump start to the essay format. Dr. Jerome Kassirer and J. R. Block were also supportive in the early going. Paul Trachtman, Scott Kim, and Doug Hofstadter generously contributed to the book. And I thank Martin Gardner for putting ambigrams into perspective in his Foreword.

I am greatly indebted to Ken Leyden of PHP Typography for donating the typographic raw material that ended up as the little aphorisms flanking each ambigram.

Many thanks to Hal Taylor for his excellent finished art of several of my ambigram drawings. Dorothy Amsden's computer-graphics skills helped make the CHANGES ambigram much more exciting than it would otherwise have been.

My wife, Lynn, always believed in "the book." Without her continuous support *Wordplay* might never have existed. In addition, her critiques of the essays and helpful suggestions were invaluable.

To all of you, thank you.

FOREWORD

In geometry, a symmetry is defined with respect to an operation that leaves a figure unchanged. For example, if a plane figure such as a capital A is not altered by mirror reflection, it is said to have mirror-reflection symmetry. If it is unchanged by turning it upside down, as Z is, it has 180-degree, or twofold, rotational symmetry. If it is unchanged by a quarter turn, as a square would be, it has 90-degree, or fourfold, rotational symmetry. An equilateral triangle has 60-degree, or threefold, rotational symmetry. The circle is so rich in symmetry that it is unchanged by reflection or by any degree of turning.

It would be interesting to know when it was first discovered that certain printed words are unchanged when inverted or reflected. Were the Greeks and Romans aware of such whimsies? Recognizing that English words such as SWIMS are the same upside-down must be as old as printing. Apparently it was not until this century that upside-down sentences were constructed, such as the swimming-pool sign "NOW NO SWIMS ON MON."

Words symmetric with respect to a vertical axis, such as TUT TUT, are unchanged by a mirror placed at either end. Words symmetric with respect to a horizontal axis, such as CODEBOOK, are unchanged by a mirror held above or below. Some words have vertical symmetry axes when printed vertically, such as AUTOMATA and the owl's palindromic statement TOO HOT TO HOOT. These would be unaltered by a mirror on either side.

It was not until about two decades ago that here and there a few individuals discovered how to take words and phrases and, by subtly distorting them, give them a symmetry they otherwise would not possess. It is easy to see that WOW is MOM upside-down, but who would have guessed that an enormous variety of words and phrases with no symmetry when printed could be shaped so they were the same when inverted or reflected, or changed to an entirely different word or phrase? So accustomed are we to discerning the meaning of a word by an awareness of its overall pattern that its pattern can undergo amazingly severe distortions and still be immediately recognized. The earliest (and somewhat crude) instances of this kind of wordplay known to me were on a page of *The Strand,* a British monthly, Volume 36, 1908, page 117, where "chump," "honey," and the signature of W. H. Hill are so scripted that they are the same upside-down.

Although occasionally an artist or calligrapher would hit on an example of this kind of sorcery, it was three men who recently developed this curious technique to an incredible level of perfection. Scott Kim is the best known because of the publicity he received in Scot Morris's *Omni* column and in my "Mathematical Games" column in *Scientific American,* and because of his beautiful book *Inversions* (Scott's name for ambigrams) and his MacPaint™ computer disk with its instruction book, *Letterforms and Illusion.* Kim's friend Douglas Hofstadter, of *Gödel, Escher, Bach* fame, began working the same field at about the same time. His book *Ambigrammi* has so far been published only in Italy. The third man, who started ambigramming back in 1973, is John Langdon, whose marvelous book you now hold.

"Ambigram" is an appropriate term because it suggests a broader property than "symmetry." Some ambigrams are not ambiguous with respect to symmetry, such as words and phrases that become other words and phrases when inverted, and ambigrams that are ambiguous with respect to a figure and its background. With the latter, your mind alternates between two gestalts, like trying to decide if a skirt is blue with white stripes or white with blue stripes. A couple of that type appear in Langdon's Preface.

Word ambigrams of all types are distant cousins of picture ambigrams such as faces that turn into other faces when inverted, or landscapes (some painted by Salvador Dali) that become faces after a quarter turn. The rabbit-duck, a familiar figure to psychologists, is a rabbit one way and a duck after a 90-degree turn. (Three-dimensional rabbit-ducks were made in pottery by the Weller company; you can find them in antique shows.)

Other well-known ambiguous pictures include the young-lady-or-old-woman, depending on which gestalt locks into your brain, and pictures that are one scene when looked at close up and a different picture when viewed from far away. Shigeo Fukuda, a Japanese sculptor, makes statues that are, for instance, a piano player when seen from one angle and a violin player when seen from a different angle.

The cartoonist George Carlson contributed dozens of upside-down pictures to *John Martin's Book,* a children's monthly that flourished in the 1920s. Several books of such pictures have been published, notably Rex Whistler's *¡OHO!* and the *Topsys and Turvys* books of Peter Newell. From 1903 to 1904, a cartoonist named Gustave Verbeek drew a Sunday comic for the *New York Herald.* You followed the story by taking its panels in order, then turned it upside down and continued the story by taking the same panels in reverse order! This was made possible by the fact that a character called Little Lady Lovekins turned into Old Man Mufaroo when inverted, and vice versa. Maybe someday an artist skilled in upside-down pictures will collaborate with a designer of John Langdon's mysterious talents on a book of pictures with captions that change, like the pictures, when the book is inverted.

Langdon has included a "How-to" section in this book. With

its help you can try to construct some ambigrams of your own. I warn you, it's not easy! But I can imagine no reader of this delightful, fantastic volume who cannot enjoy the magic of Langdon's creations and the Taoist insights of his commentaries.

MARTIN GARDNER

PREFACE

The first time I saw the yin and yang symbol was one of those moments that become permanent mental photographs. I didn't know back in 1966 what lay beyond the door, but it is now clear that a door had opened for me. Yin and yang made a deep and immediate impression—an impression I was aware of somewhere between my nervous system and the source of my emotions, but would have been hard pressed to identify or describe out loud. If I had said anything, I might have quoted the introduction to the TV program "Ben Casey": "Man . . . woman . . . birth . . . death . . . infinity . . . ," followed perhaps by "summer, winter, hot, cold, north, south, on, off, up, down," and so on. Although it would be several years before I ever heard of Taoism, the ancient Chinese philosophy from which yin and yang originates, I seem to have subconsciously sensed that the symbol's simple representation of polarized opposites and harmonious complements applied perfectly to most of the major forces inherent in our existence.

I thought about the yin and yang symbol and fooled around with it graphically for years, initially unaware of the interest in Oriental thought that was to grow steadily in popularity through the ensuing decades. After seeing parts of this book in its early stages, a young physics student wrote to me: "Taoist imagery of interaction and of a natural, flowing, universal holism is becoming more and more infused into our consciousness. Such ideas have been a latent part of our psyche for centuries. Their lineage can be traced, almost directly, from the Renaissance hermeticists to the alchemists and early scientists, through writers such as Eliot and Joyce, and finally into aspects of our own popular culture."

In the sixties, Ram Dass (Richard Alpert), Timothy Leary and Alan Watts experimented with realms of consciousness through the use of psychedelic drugs; Ravi Shankar and George Harrison introduced us to meditative sitar music, and the Maharishi brought us Transcendental Meditation. These were just a few of the early influences upon what has burgeoned into the cultural phenomenon now called "The New Age." Although the new subculture was more attracted to Zen philosophy, yin and yang drew me toward its ancestor, Taoism. Zen seemed to be concerned with mental discipline and mind games; Taoism was more relaxed and natural. The countercultural slogan "Go with the flow" could easily be the motto on the Taoist coat of arms.

Just out of college with a degree in English and an interest in words and art, I entered the field of advertising with no clear idea of a professional direction. It didn't take me long, however, to develop an interest in corporate logos. The simplicity and symbolism inherent in logo design appealed to me, especially when it involved the design of letters and words. Through jobs as a phototypographer and advertising designer, and through voracious study of the work of Herb Lubalin (a pioneer in the movement to regard type's ability to communicate visually as well as linguistically), I developed and refined my ability to interpret the meaning of a word within the design of the word itself. After several years in various jobs in the field of advertising design, I went into business for myself as a logo designer and lettering artist.

In the same way that the cross could be thought of as a logo for Christianity and the Star of David as a logo for Judaism, the yin and yang symbol is a logo for Taoism. As such, it is one of the best logos ever designed. A logo should communicate, in as simple and efficient a form as possible, a maximum of information about the entity it represents. And by the time I began to read about Taoism, I found to my amazement that I had already inferred virtually all that I was reading, simply by applying the ideas of polarized opposites and harmonious complements to a seemingly infinite number of situations that exist in our lives and in the workings of the universe. This, I learned, is quite appropriate to Taoism, a basic tenet of which holds that each person should find his own way. In the words of Lao-tzu, "Without leaving my house, I [can] know the whole universe."

In the early years of my career I developed a strong interest in the work of M. C. Escher. It seemed to me that he had taken the spirit of yin and yang, both graphically—the birds and fish fitting together as neatly as the halves of yin and yang—and conceptually—exploring polarities like devils and angels, night and day, and more. In addition, some of his pieces are reflections and inversions; some treat the same subject from more than one point of view. Many of his works attempt to capture the concept of infinity. It is probably no coincidence that Escher represented his ideas primarily in black and white—polarized—which is the way that the yin and yang symbol is normally shown. I work almost exclusively in black and white, as well.

Not surprisingly, I tried to do with words what Escher had done with buildings, birds and fish. My early attempts were figure / ground reversals and were, I felt, quite unattractive and hard to read, but they undoubtedly led to my "discovery" of the potential to design words in such a way that they could be read both right side up and upside down. This new ability excited me greatly, and I was inspired to try to accomplish the feat with virtually any word or name that entered my head.

This development did not begin to reach a state of maturity, however, until I focused my attention on words that described those many natural balances and opposites with which Taoism and, indeed, much of Western science concern themselves—the words that are shown in this book as ambigrams.

IT SEEMS LIKELY that Taoism developed in much the same way as the physical sciences did—through observation of the world around us. Sir Isaac Newton is perhaps best known for his third law, which states, "For every action, there is opposed an equal and opposite reaction." The yin and yang symbol may as well have been designed to illustrate that idea. In his letter to me, the physics student also said, "Science has directly encountered [the yin / yang] theme in the study of dynamical systems, popularly termed 'chaos theory.' Chaotic behavior . . . is dependent on a feedback mechanism, in which each of several factors interact to determine the value of the others. It can be said that fractals are none other than microscopic images, resolvable to infinite but never ultimate detail, of the interaction between yin and yang." "Chaos" may not be the best name for this relatively new area of scientific study. The subjects of its interest have indeed long appeared to be chaotic, but as they begin to be understood, they exhibit instead a different kind of order—one that has eluded classical scientific methods. Yin-and-yang-like relationships are beginning to emerge between, for example, order and disorder, and stability and instability.

I began to investigate other basic scientific principles and often found either visual representations of data, such as the "normal bell curve," or descriptions of visible physical phenomena, like wave patterns. A path worn by a random sampling of a population walking across an open area of grass, for instance, not only describes a "path" of least resistance, but its depression into the earth is virtually a normal distribution curve, albeit an inverted one, caused by the majority of people walking down the middle of it. The spiral is frequently found in patterns that nature creates, from the microscopic DNA helix through snail shells and sunflowers to galaxies thousands of light years across. Often the shapes and proportions of these spirals mathematically follow the Fibonacci series: 1, 1, 2, 3, 5, 8, 13, 21, etc. Waves seem similar to a series of normal distribution curves, and the infinity symbol could be seen as two normal bell curves curled around and linked to complete a circuit. They all seem graphically, philosophically and scientifically related to one another *and* to the yin and yang symbol. They all appealed to me in the same way that yin and yang had—as simple and beautiful shapes that represented basic and powerful universal principles. Naturally, the names of these symbols and concepts became candidates for word designs that might illuminate the ideas they represent and demonstrate their relationships to the overriding yin and yang principle. Thus they became ambigrams.

It is important to me that we allow these words to escape from the limitations of a single interpretation. "Inertia," for instance, is used almost exclusively to refer to a motionless object in the process of remaining motionless. But that is only half of the story. It is also the state of a moving object continuing to move. Motion and motionlessness are as visibly opposite as black and white, but the word "inertia" yokes them together. It is a syzygy, a linguistic yin and yang.

Ambiguity is not the same as vagueness. The word refers to the fact that an idea *can* be understood in more than one way. I have tried to represent these words and the positive aspects of their ambiguities. The ability to look at something from more than one point of view is, I believe, a necessary foundation for all creativity.

THE IMPORTANCE OF ambigrams is not merely to entertain and amaze, although they seem to perform those tasks well. By doing so, however, they also present familiar concepts in an unfamiliar way and thus stimulate the reader's imagination to reconsider the familiar in a new light. Each ambigram should be digested slowly so that it can be appreciated on visual, linguistic, scientific and philosophical levels. It is my belief that by looking at everything that happens in life in the light of the yin and yang principle (which for me encompasses the principles attached to the normal bell curve, waves, the spiral and the infinity symbol) one can gain a sense of trust in the order of the universe, and not be disheartened by the appearance of chaos that a closeup view often provides.

You don't need to leave your room.
Remain sitting at your table and listen.
Don't even listen, simply wait.
Don't even wait.
Be quite still and solitary.
The world will freely offer itself to you.
To be unmasked, it has no choice.
It will roll in ecstasy at your feet.

—Franz Kafka,
THE GREAT WALL OF CHINA

INTRODUCTION

THIS BOOK IS an illusion. It's something other than
what it may seem to be at first glance. Or maybe
even second glance. Initially it may appear to be a
book of unusual lettering art. But soon after, the
reader may discover that there is more here than
meets the eye. It is a book of optical illusions. It is
a book of

There are puns, semantic acrobatics and typographic gymnastics as well. The latter are known as
ambigrams (*ambi-* : both + *-gram* : letter)—words

that can be read in more than one way or from more than a single vantage point. The word "wordplay," above, is one kind of ambigram, and by turning the book upside down, you'll get an idea of what this wordplay is all about.

Ambigrams come in a number of forms, limited only by the ambigrammist's imagination, and usually involve some kind of symmetry. This book is made up of three types:

1. words with rotational symmetry, like the one above. Most of the ambigrams in this book fall into this category.

2. words that have bilateral, or mirror-image, symmetry. If the reader could see through the backs of the pages these are printed on, they could be read from both sides of the page *without* turning the book upside down. Their duality, as it is presented here, may be observed in a mirror reflection. On *very* rare occasions a word may be designed in such a way as to read the same with both rotational and mirror-image symmetry. It would seem that this would be the ideal ambigram, and indeed it is just that. My good friend and fellow ambigrammist Bob Petrick designed this ambigram, which is perfectly symmetrical along both horizontal and vertical axes. The word CHOICE on page 81 and the CHOICE / DECIDE network that follows

it also reflect this double symmetry, but those are also examples of a third type of ambigram, which I call

   3. chains. These are ambigrams that cannot stand alone as single words, but depend on being linked to the preceding and ensuing words. In a chain-style ambigram there is an overlap of one or more letters providing the linkage. Chains can be made up of ambigrams of either of the above-mentioned types. THESIS and ANTITHESIS (page 13), NO LIMITATIONS (page 155), and NEVERENDING (page 173) are examples of rotational chains. Most appropriate to this form is the CHAIN REACTION network on page 97. PAST and FUTURE on pages 72–73 represent a bilateral chain.

EACH AMBIGRAM REPRESENTS a kind of simultaneity in that two things (usually two representations of the same word) occupy the same space at the same time. On a broader plane, ambigrams demonstrate another kind of simultaneity: the same thing happening at the same time in different places. When I first discovered the ability to turn words on their heads, I thought I must have come upon something totally new and unique. Not only have I come across several historical examples since then, many of which are touched on in Martin Gardner's Foreword, but there are now, to my knowledge, in the United States, at least half a dozen of us who are seriously devoting our time to forcing words to read in more than one way. Each of us seems to have come upon the idea quite independently, and, happily, each of us approaches it from a very different direction.

IN A WAY, this book is an inversion, too. It is a

reversal

of what we expect a book to be. Books are generally a lot of little words strung together, eventually revealing an overall idea. Often the little words are illustrated by visual material. In this case the overall idea *is* the visual material, the visual material is words, and the little strung-together words "illustrate" the visual matter.

In most cases, the "illustrations" are my personal reflections on each word, its meaning, and the application or relevance of the idea behind the word to our everyday lives. The first few essays, accompanying the PHILOSOPHY, SCIENCE, YIN & YANG, SYNTHESIS, AMBIGUITY and SYMMETRY ambigrams, lay the foundations for an understanding and an enjoyment of all the ambigrams and essays. They describe, in a way, "where I'm coming from." Several essays explore directly the ideas of Taoism and its relationship to the basic precepts of modern physics, and occasionally tie those together with ambigrams. It should be noted that my expertise in the various sciences referred to is limited indeed. I had one course in physics in tenth grade and remember from it only the concept and beauty of wave patterns. My love for the normal bell curve is the sole remnant of an introductory psychology course. In the realm of science I am, in the truest sense of the word, an amateur. I love the basic precepts of physics particularly, not only for their pure and simple inherent beauty, but also because they can be seen and experienced in everyday life.

Some of the essays are responses to the particular word as seen from an unusual point of view. Some are playful throughout, others only here and there; it's hard for me to let the opportunity for a pun go by simply because of the context or even because it may be "bad."

In a few cases, others who are interested in words and ambigrams have contributed to the book. Douglas Hofstadter sheds light on the word "syzygy," Scott Kim makes algebra into a stimulating game, and Scott's friend Paul Trachtman takes a unique and poetic look at balance.

My hope is that the reader will find that the essays provide examples of the kind of inspiration everyone might take from the ambigrams themselves.

ULTIMATELY, THIS IS a book of

Philosophy

The ideas contained herein have been developing in me on a conscious level for the past twenty years. They provide stability and meaning for my life. The ambigrams have not inspired the philosophy. Rather they are the natural result of the philosophy coming to rest in the mind of an artist who loves words.

"Philosophy is written in this grand book—I mean the universe—which stands continually open to our gaze, but it cannot be understood unless one first learns to comprehend the language and interpret the characters in which it is written."

galileo

—after *Il Saggiatore* (1623)

AS A PROFESSIONAL lettering artist, I have two primary require- ments of an ambigram: it should be readable and it should be attractive. In addition, I think that an ambigram reaches its greatest potential when it provokes thought beyond a mere appreciation of its symmetry—when there is a resonant rela- tionship between the word, its meaning and its "ambi-graphic" representation.

THE DEVELOPMENT OF an ambigram begins with exploration and play, taking place as doodling on a layout pad. Usually I will have been thinking about a number of ideas within a general category—more often than not an aspect of the physical sciences and its relationship to natural opposites and balances, for ex- ample, the universal force of electromagnetism and some related concepts: positive and negative, north and south polarities, and so on. I would play with the words "electricity," "electron," "magnet," "magnetic," and "magnetism," "polarity," "polar," "polarized," and so forth. All of these mental gymnastics seemed to me to be a kind of graphic artist's philosophical indulgence, so, of course, I *had* to play with the word "philosophy." Perhaps appropriately, it turned out to be my favorite ambigram.

In order to save the time, effort and continual disorientation of turning my pad of layout paper upside down, I have become fairly proficient at writing upside down and backwards. Each word is written, in the beginning, in a single pen stroke and in straightforward capital letters.

PHILOSOPHY   GRAVITY   MAGNETIC

If a word is likely to work as an ambigram, it almost always depends on some letters being natural reverses of either themselves or other letters. These provide support for the letters that require more distortion and manipulation and might, out of context, be difficult to read. In the word PHILOSOPHY, the OSO in the middle is an optimistic sign, as are the Hs near either end. The A and V would be a natural starting point in the word GRAVITY. In MAGNETIC, the N in the middle will work, but nothing else looks helpful right away.

Let's follow the development of the PHILOSOPHY ambigram. We now have the OSO and the Hs, so we need to concentrate on making a P that, when reversed, could read as a Y, and an IL that could function as a P.

First the P-Y situation. Nothing too obvious here, but we do know that a lowercase Y can be drawn with a loop at the bottom that *Y* might form the protruding bowl of the P, and since the Y comes at the end of the word, perhaps the loop can be somewhat exaggerated in size. This would form the most important characteristic of a P, and as the P is the initial character, the exaggeration could allow it to be bigger than the other letters, as an initial capital often is. Now the upside-down P offers no suggestions for the split top that is necessary to create a Y. But in a more flourished handwriting style, the Y almost necessarily creates a fancier cursive P, and now we see a way *P* of getting the Y to work: a script capital P would conceivably have some extraneous material to the left of the main stroke, and by continuing the round stroke of the P through and beyond the back stroke, we have created a reasonably credible Y.

Making the IL into another P may be a bit more difficult. Not only do we have to make both Ps believable within the same design, but we also have to make one letter into two letters, and vice versa. In a case like this we have to look at individual strokes, not just whole letters. There are two main, vertical strokes in the IL and a subordinate horizontal stroke. In some forms of the letter P there is one predominant vertical with a subordinate vertical attached to it by two connectors, one of which is often minimized in typeface design and sometimes even omitted. And since an I, in the lowercase form, is shorter than an L, maybe the P *can* be made from an I and an L.

Things seem to be working out fairly well, but note that all the manipulations we've been through have guided us toward lowercase forms, whereas we started out with all capital letters. Designing an ambigram is not like designing a typeface. In the design of a typeface, each letter must perform well, functionally and aesthetically, on either side of every other letter in the alphabet. I call this an "open system." An ambigram is a "closed system." The letters that are drawn for one specific ambigram may not even be recognizable outside the context of that ambigram. This allows the artist significant latitude beyond the rules of everyday typography. For instance, it might be necessary to mix capital and lowercase forms. Nevertheless, readability will be best served if we can avoid breaking any more rules than necessary.

At the moment we have

PHIJOSOΠHY

We're getting there, but it's still not exactly easy to read or particularly attractive. It looks a little like Greek, with some letters recognizable and others not, but while that may be appropriate to the origins of the word (*philos* : love + *sophia* : wisdom), it's not much help in achieving readability in English. Even though it means sacrificing those very important and easy-to-read Hs, I think we're going to have to try moving to all lowercase. The OSO is great because oso works just as well. We just have to get an upside-down lowercase h that also looks like a right-side-up lowercase h. Fortunately, we're in luck. Those earlier decisions that led us toward more cursive, slightly flourishy forms have created a format within which a more cursive, slightly flourishy h will be right at home.

Now we're in business. All that remains between here and a finished ambigram is a decision on style. It is here that critical judgment will determine the readability and attractiveness of the design. In most ambigrams, the necessary manipulations leave a fairly narrow range of stylistic choices. On occasion the basic structure of an ambigram works so simply and so well that a greater range is afforded, and in that event, I try to instill a stylistic flavor appropriate to the meaning of the word. Rarely, as in the case of the ELECTRICITY design on page 39, an almost pictorially symbolic style will actually help the readability and success of the ambigram.

The fact that the IL-and-P combination depended on the traditional placement of thicker and thinner strokes, combined with the fact that some weight variation is natural to a cursive lettering style, and finally, the fact that weight variation helps in readability—especially where some of the letters are less recognizable than usual—leads to the inescapable conclusion that a monoweight style would be a counterproductive choice.

So from here on, all the experimentations use letterforms that show some variation in weight.

As it turns out, the experiments in which the thick and thin strokes tend toward extremes seem a little more difficult to read, so although the weight variation is important, we'll keep it on the minimal side.

Once the style has been determined in thumbnail-sketch form, it is photographically enlarged to provide the basis of a large, very careful and accurate drawing done by hand, with pencil. That drawing is transferred to inking paper. French curves, oval templates and other instruments may be used to outline the letterforms so that they are smooth and clean. Once half the word has been completed, two identical photographic prints are made, pasted together and then rephotographed to provide a single piece of art ready for reproduction.

". . . the books are something like our books,
only the words go the wrong way . . ."

—Lewis Carroll, THROUGH THE LOOKING GLASS

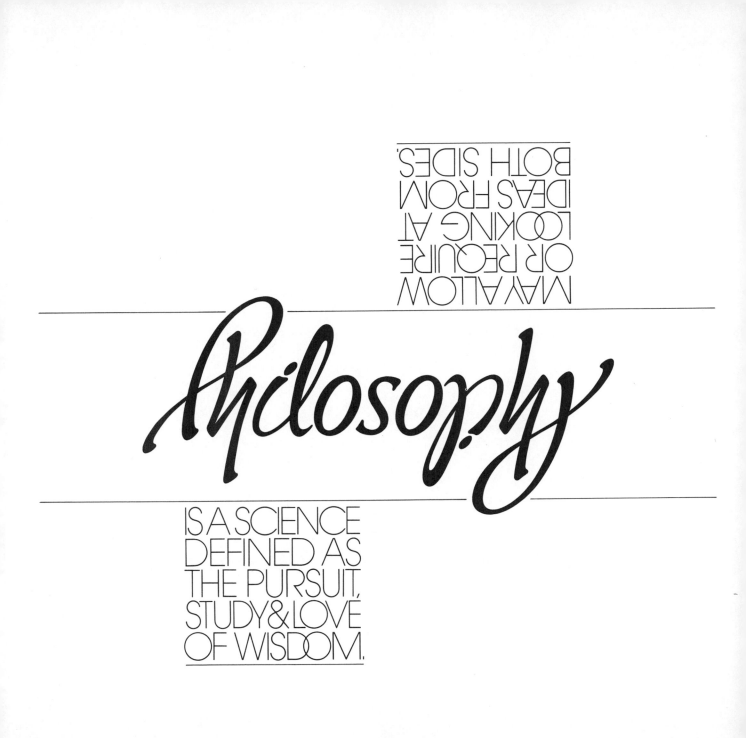

MAY ALLOW
OR REQUIRE
LOOKING AT
IDEAS FROM
BOTH SIDES.

Philosophy

IS A SCIENCE
DEFINED AS
THE PURSUIT,
STUDY & LOVE
OF WISDOM.

PHILOSOPHY & SCIENCE

But what after all are man's truths?

They are his irrefutable errors.

THE JOYFUL WISDOM
Friedrich Wilhelm Nietzsche

THE SEARCH FOR truth is an excellent example of the infinite. It will be pursued forever and never attained. This is due to certain factors built into the attitudes and *modi operandi* of those who seek to define truth: philosophers, scientists and artists.

The processes of philosophy require that strict logic must be adhered to and that conventions of argument must be followed. For example, "If A is true, then it must follow that B is also true." Or "Since A is true, C cannot be true." A philosophical idea must be supported by logic and is likely to be subjected to challenge from another logical construct, another point of view. In general, philosophers do not attempt to

I

establish immutable truths. The field seems to accept that there will always be another person with a new approach to "The Truth." As the word "philosophy" implies with its root meaning, "a love of wisdom," the process is all-important. It's the approach that counts.

The root of the word "science," on the other hand, is the Latin word meaning "to know." Historically, science has tried to reach conclusions. But the standards for acceptance are much more rigorous. Scientists attempt to ascertain their truths through hypothesis, experiment, deduction and proof. A hypothesis often meets its ultimate test in the practice of disproof. It may be supported by any number of experiments, but if it can be disproved as well, it cannot be thought of as a truth, no matter how logical.

When a hypothesis has been proved and cannot be disproved, it may be thought of as being true, for the time being, at least. The trick is that scientists will use the word "hypothesis" where laymen would use the word "theory." Strong hypotheses, supported by successful experiments, can build a "theory"—an interlocking set of laws that explain certain phenomena. When verified, theories are accepted as "provisionally true." Science is willing to replace "truths" with newer "truths."

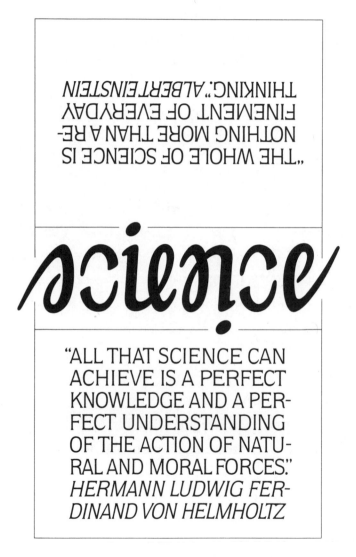

"THE WHOLE OF SCIENCE IS NOTHING MORE THAN A RE-FINEMENT OF EVERYDAY THINKING." ALBERT EINSTEIN

science

"ALL THAT SCIENCE CAN ACHIEVE IS A PERFECT KNOWLEDGE AND A PER-FECT UNDERSTANDING OF THE ACTION OF NATU-RAL AND MORAL FORCES." *HERMANN LUDWIG FER-DINAND VON HELMHOLTZ*

Each new truth exposes new information, which raises new questions, and thereby engenders new hypotheses. With the demands made upon scientific process and the acceptance that truths may be only temporary, we see once again that Ultimate Truths are something of a Holy Grail. As J. Bronowski says in *Science and Human Values,* "Science is not a mechanism but a human progress, and not a set of findings but the search for them."

Completing the equilateral triangle of truth seekers are the artists. Bronowski goes on: "The creative act is alike in art as in science; but it cannot be identical in the two; there must be a difference as well as a likeness. . . . The artist in his creation surely has open to him a dimension of freedom which is closed to the scientist." Whereas scientists are careful to use strict controls to ensure the accuracy of their data and findings, artists are free to approach truths by any path, with no expectation of following what was done before. Artists can hardly expect *not* to follow, as it is too late to precede, but they try not to be led, at least. They often proceed by way of a synthesizing process, looking not to the recent past but to a more distant antecedent to blend with their own very current ideas. Thus the viewer looks at something familiar in a completely different way. This is the case with the ambigrams in this book: they pull together ancient philosophies, traditional science and modern typographic design. Their goal is to engender a new point of view toward words that may have long been familiar.

Bronowski's philosophy brings the separate fields of science and art together: "Science is nothing else than the search to discover unity in the wild variety of nature—or more exactly, in the variety of our experience." Quoting Coleridge's definition of beauty, "unity in variety," Bronowski says, "The arts are the same search. . . . Each in its own way looks for likenesses under the variety of human experience." Describing science as a creative endeavor, he says, "In the act of creation, a man brings together two facets of reality and, by discovering a likeness between them, makes them one. This act is the same in Leonardo, in Keats and in Einstein. And the spectator who is moved by the finished work of art or the scientific theory re-lives the same discovery; his appreciation also is a re-creation."

In art, the well-worn path is to be avoided lest the product be considered craft. But the goal of art has never been to establish truth, only to provide more views of it. Since another look at reality is produced every minute, the process will never be complete. In the visual arts, as in science, there will always be another way of looking at things.

In philosophy, science and art, it is the process that is important. The processes provide us with temporary truths that, since each moment of reality is only temporary itself, ought to be satisfactory for the time being. All that can really be done is to record and organize human experience. But that's all right—it gives artists, scientists and philosophers something to do. ■

YIN AND YANG

THE YIN AND yang symbol is central to the ancient Chinese philosophy of Taoism. It shows a balanced, reflected pair of complementary opposites symbolizing the dynamic balance of opposing forces.

Virtually everything we know can be seen in terms of opposing or complementary halves. Time can be divided into day and night, space into north and south, human beings into male and female.

To the originators of Taoism, the black yin represented the female, darkness, inwardness, yielding, and the unknown, while the white yang symbolized the male, light, protrusion, aggressiveness, and the overt.

Since none of these entities could exist without the other, each is necessarily an aspect of the other. To be more accurate, each yin and each yang is an integral aspect or part of a greater whole: "yinandyang"—or the Tao.

From this point of view we can look at *everything* as being divisible into equally valid aspects: everything is made up of matter and anti-matter; matter can be divided into living and non-living matter, living matter into human and non-human, human into male and female, and so on, down to a subatomic level.

Yin and yang looks fluid, and indeed it is quite flexible. Taking it to an extreme but thought-provoking point of view, philosopher Alan Watts said that at times he felt that he was yang and the entire rest of the universe was yin.

As a pendulum changes its course when it has reached the extreme point of its swing in one direction, so yang begins at the tiny point where yin reaches its maximum width. Immediately following the "longest day of the year," June 22, the days begin to get "shorter." How far can you walk into the woods? Only halfway. After that, you're walking out.

Immediately adjacent to the point where yang begins, in the middle of the maximum width of yin, is a dot of white. This

POLARIZED OPPOSITES

Yin & Yang

HARMONIOUS
COMPLEMENTS

signifies the idea that the very act of reaching a maximum point creates the seed of an opposite reaction. Another way of looking at this idea would demonstrate that in a complementary relationship between entities, the total elimination of one by the other is impossible. Because it is light that creates darkness, in the form of shadows, light cannot ever do away with all darkness (unless perhaps someday—and it would be day!—all mass is converted to light energy). It would be impossible for a predator species to devour all of its prey. As the population of the prey dwindled to the point where the members of the predator species could not be fed, the predators would begin to die off, reversing the trend. Soon the population of the prey species would begin to increase. An all-and-nothing relationship can be approached, but yin and yang's natural tendency toward balance prevents it from being achieved.

While the complementary "halves" may not necessarily appear to be equal, eventually most of them do turn out that way. Day and night are equal amounts of time only twice a year, at the equinoxes. But over the course of a year, every place on earth has day half of the time and night half of the time. Yin and yang can function as a graph in which complementary relationships are described.

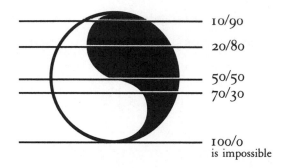

10/90
20/80
50/50
70/30

100/0
is impossible

Much of the time the complementary opposites exist in a dominant-and-subordinate relationship. But yin and yang is never static. Sociological research may show a majority point of view continuing to grow in popularity, but eventually the human instinct for individuality will react and a countermovement will arise. The social upheaval of the sixties was in direct response not only to the overt oppression of blacks and the thinly veiled oppression of women, but also to the enormous acceptance of the fifties' postwar values. Conformity, convenience and anti-communism were so thoroughly ingrained in American society that they became oppressive to many of the nation's young people. Oppression always breeds rebellion. So natural is this instinct that, for the most part, things tend not to shift to extremes. The need for relative stability and balance usually keeps things hovering in a range near the center, but the greater the trend in one direction, the more extreme the response will be.

Yin and yang represents nature's ability to keep things in balance in a constantly shifting process of give-and-take. ∎

A stated proposition;
a theme offered to be
defended & debated,
proved or disproved

thesisthesisthesis
sisthesisthesisthe
hesisthesisthesis
isthesisthesisthes
thesisthesisthesisthesisth
sisthesisthesisthesisthesis

antithesisantithesisantithesisantith
sisantithesisantithesisantithesisant
hesisantithesisantit
titthesisantithesisan
antithesisantithesis
sisantithesisantithe

A counter-thesis; a
contrasting idea or
point of view in op-
position to a thesis

THESIS: THE SUN is the source of all life. Antithesis: God is the giver of all life. Synthesis: God is the sun. The sun is God.

Dictionaries define "thesis" as "a proposition, an affirmation," and "a postulate." "Antithesis" is defined as "a contrast, an opposition, a contrary." These definitions are, perhaps appropriately, oriented toward the area of debate. The word "thesis" is seldom heard outside of an academic arena, but it is not uncommon to hear someone say that one thing is the "antithesis" of another: "Science is the antithesis of art," "Love is the antithesis of hate," and more. While the content of these examples may be debatable, they represent our instinctive need to

and antithesis, result-
ing in an ideal whole.

A combination of ele-
ments from the thesis

define and understand one thing in terms of another. Every yin is the antithesis of a complementary yang. In a debate, as on the facing page, each thesis in a series of theses can be met and countered by an anti-thesis.

This opposition between thesis and antithesis could be graphically represented  by a black rectangle and a white rectangle of equal size adjacent to each other. But this describes a static situation in which the tension inherent in the relationship is never resolved. Like participants in many arguments, neither has any effect on the other. There is no winner, no loser, no give-and-take. There is nothing learned or agreed upon—in short, there is no synthesis.

Synthesis is a combination of separate elements into a complete whole.  The only way we could picture a combination of the rectangles above would result in something that, in a debate, neither side would be likely to find very satisfying: gray—a compromise. When the opposites of thesis and antithesis are pictured as yin and as yang, however, they fit together in a very satisfying composite whole, with both sides retaining their characteristics and integrity.

Art is the antithesis of science. They are fundamentally different. The scientific method proceeds from the left hemisphere of the brain, moving methodically, each step based upon the data from the preceding step. Art emanates from the right hemisphere and, not constrained by logic, is propelled by intuition and imaginative association. Yet while their individual characteristics vary greatly, art and science are essentially the same. Each is a process involving the observation of phenomena in order to describe and understand the world around us.

Thesis: art. Antithesis: science. Synthesis: da Vinci. ■

AMBIGUITY

In JOHN GODFREY Saxe's well-known poem "The Blind Men and the Elephant," the six blind men of Indostan all went to learn what an elephant was like. Each approached the beast from a different direction and felt in turn the elephant's side, its tusk, its trunk, its leg, its ear, and its tail. Relating their experiences to the familiar, the six compared the elephant to, respectively, a wall, a spear, a snake, a tree, a fan, and a rope.

> And so these men of Indostan
>   Disputed loud and long,
> Each in his own opinion
>   Exceeding stiff and strong,
> Though each was partly in the right,
>   And all were in the wrong!

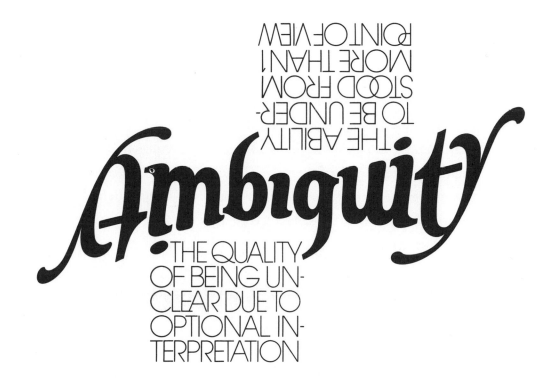

Ambiguity

THE ABILITY TO BE UNDER-STOOD FROM MORE THAN 1 POINT OF VIEW.

THE QUALITY OF BEING UN-CLEAR DUE TO OPTIONAL IN-TERPRETATION

We have often heard that if there are ten witnesses to a crime, they'll provide ten differing accounts, none of which may be incorrect. When I imagine this situation, I picture the witnesses spread randomly around in a circle with the incident taking place in the middle. Their accounts are transcribed from their memories as if they were each describing a photograph they had taken at the same moment. If they had, each photograph would, of course, be a two-dimensional representation of the scene from a single point of view. When all the photographs are blended into a composite, a more three-dimensional, and therefore more "real," picture would result. This is exactly what the cubists were attempting to do when they painted different, overlapping views of the same object—they felt that they were providing a more "real" representation of reality than the "realistic" images of painters of the past, as well as those that were emanating from the relatively new field of photography. (Eventually, photography would use a similar approach in creating a holographic image.)

We use the word "ambiguity" to describe a situation that can be understood from more than one point of view. Following the example above, it would be fair to say that every situation—all reality—is ambiguous. Most of us respond to ambiguities and cubist paintings in the same way. We don't understand them, so we retreat from them. But it would seem that the more ambiguity there is, the more accurate the description of reality can be. We should, therefore, if we really want to understand the world around us, embrace ambiguity and always try to see a situation from as many different points of view as possible.

Generally, people don't want to have to see things from other points of view. It's so much easier to live with our "two-dimensional photographs." And yet ambiguity is actually built into our physical makeup so that we *can* understand our surroundings. Each of our two eyes sees a slightly different image. The brain takes these two images and synthesizes them into a single picture, one of the important features of which is the perception of depth, and this would not be the case were we to have but one eye. This phenomenon has been dramatically demonstrated over the past several generations through stereopticons, Viewmasters, and 3-D movie glasses. In each of these, two different two-dimensional images seen separately by two eyes take on the appearance of three dimensions.

Reality is ambiguous. Ambiguity is synthesis. The problem and the solution are one. ∎

SYMMETRY

SYMMETRY IS DEFINED in *Webster's New Collegiate Dictionary*, 1961 edition, as: "1: due or balanced proportion; beauty of form arising from such harmony 2: correspondence in size, shape, and relative position of parts on opposite sides of a dividing line or median plane." Preceding the first definition is the notation "*now rare.*" And even the second definition is much broader in scope than the way we use the word in common speech. The word "symmetry" is normally used these days to refer to one specific type of symmetry: a mirrored similarity on either side of a vertical center line. Like several of the words in this book, "symmetry" has suffered from a narrowing of its definition.

THE BEAUTY OF AN ENTIRETY, WHICH ORIGINATES FROM THE HARMONY OF ITS COMPONENTS.

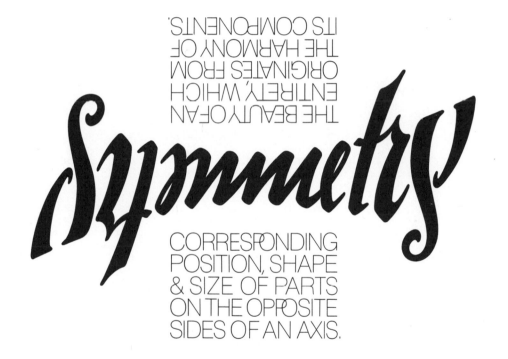

CORRESPONDING POSITION, SHAPE & SIZE OF PARTS ON THE OPPOSITE SIDES OF AN AXIS.

When William Blake wrote,

> Tyger, tyger, burning bright
> In the forests of the night,
> What immortal hand or eye
> Could frame thy fearful symmetry?

he was probably not indulging in hyperbole over the fact that the tiger's body was the same on both the left and right sides. More in line with Webster's first definition, he meant that the tiger is a marvelous piece of work, and a quite beautiful one at that.

Taking the second definition, we find there are a number of types of symmetry. The left-right symmetry referred to is called mirror-image symmetry. In this book, only BALANCE and WATERFALLS represent this type of symmetry. Most of the ambigrams in this book, including SYMMETRY on the previous page, are examples of rotational symmetry. Rather than looking the same when viewed in a mirror, they look the same when turned 180 degrees. While this may not be what we normally think of as symmetry, its symmetry *can* be demonstrated. In a two-step process, an image of rotational symmetry can be achieved by producing a vertical mirror image, and then a horizontal mirror image of that vertical image.

step 1   step 2

Following the shadow that begins on the bottom and right side of each letter from one step to the next makes it easier to see these two stages.

The point is that there is a lot more symmetry around than we might think. In his book *Das Energi* Paul Williams says it this way:

> Truth is what sounds right.
> Beauty is what looks right.
> Beware of Symmetry.
>
> Beware means be aware.

■

REFLECT

SEEING THINGS FROM a different point of view may only mean looking in a different direction. Like back instead of forward. Today I caught myself looking back on an experience in which I caught myself looking back.

I walked into the hotel bathroom, clicked on the light and stood at the counter. No more than three feet away, I saw a familiar face. The recognition seemed to be mutual. "Of course," I thought, "it's only my own image in the glass." Everything seemed perfect . . . symmetrical. The hair color was right, the eyes were the same, even the teeth. When I moved my mouth the image moved its mouth. My eyebrow, its eyebrow. Not a moment later,

MUSE OR MEDITATE.
TICULAR SUBJECT; TO
THOUGHTS TO A PAR-
TO TURN BACK ONE'S

TO TURN BACK, TO RE-
DIRECT MOTION IN THE
OPPOSITE DIRECTION;
TO ACT AS A MIRROR.

either—in the same instant! Was the person in the mirror *thinking* the same thing? Was he wondering about me? I leaned a little to one side. In the mirror across from me, I could see the mirror behind me across the room. In the mirror behind me, I saw the image of my image in the mirror in front of me. It was looking at the image across from it and appeared to be wondering whether it was thinking the same thoughts. But I couldn't make eye contact with it. It was concentrating on another familiar image across from it in the mirror in the mirror in the mirror. Reflections on reflections. Odd infinitum! ■

BALANCE

Imagination . . . reveals itself in the balance
or reconciliation of opposite or
discordant qualities.

BIOGRAPHIA LITERARIA
Samuel Taylor Coleridge

THE OXFORD ENGLISH DICTIONARY looks at the verb "to balance" from two slightly different points of view. The word can mean "to weigh two things physically"; it can also mean "to weigh or consider two ideas"—"to ponder or deliberate." In a way, then, balancing is what we're doing in this book: evaluating different points of view.

The Bible is more specific. The book of Ecclesiastes admonishes us to "weigh thy words in balance." In the following poem, Paul Trachtman balances not only his words, but He with She and left-brained scientific knowledge against right-brained associative logic.

29

HE SAID, "Balance is all in the mind."
SHE SAID, "The organ of balance is in the inner ear."
AND HE SAID, "Therefore, the mind is located in the inner ear."

If you want to know balance, practice imbalance.
Here are some simple exercises:
Put one foot in your mouth, and stand on it.
Eat your words for one week. Try to provide a balanced diet.
Speak out of both sides of your mouth, and explain that it is
only a balancing act.

The way to keep your balance is to keep losing it.
To get anywhere, lose your balance.
Walking is the act of falling in small steps,
by pulling one foot out from under you at a time.
To stay put, lose your balance.
Standing still is the illusion you are not moving,
created by starting to fall in all directions
and constantly changing your mind.
Balance is not the absence of imbalance, but its essence.

HE SAID, "Balance is all in the mind."
SHE SAID, "The body knows how to balance itself."
AND HE SAID, "Therefore, the body is located in the mind."

■

BALANCE IS NOT A RIGID STATE OF STATIC SYMMETRY IS A PROCESS OF CONSTANT ADJUSTMENT

I hated to think of an upside-down tightrope walker, so this ambigram is a mirror image.

POLARIZED

At the very roots of Chinese thinking
and feeling there lies the principle of polarity,
which is not to be confused with the ideas of opposition
or conflict. In the metaphors of other cultures,
light is at war with darkness,
life with death, good with evil, and the positive with
the negative, and thus an idealism to cultivate
the former and be rid of the latter
flourishes throughout much of the world.
To the traditional way of Chinese thinking,
this is as incomprehensible as an electric current without
both positive and negative poles, for polarity
is the principle that $+$ and $-$, north and south, are
different aspects of the same system,
and that the disappearance of either one of them
would be the disappearance of the system.

TAO: THE WATERCOURSE WAY
Alan Watts

32

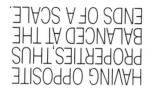

polarized

HAVING MOVED TO
POSITIONS OF THE
GREATEST POSSI-
BLE DIVERGENCE.

Taoism avoids value judgments. Yang is not better than yin any more than south is better than north. They're relative. And relatives. On the other hand, we seem to think that good is better than bad. Yet this can be true only in a way made possible by defining something in comparative terms of itself. "Good" and "bad" have to be thought of as relative terms in order to have any real meaning for us. Taken as absolutes, we could hardly apply them to anything that happens in our lives. Every silver lining has a cloud, and vice versa.

Sometimes words take on value judgments. In the sciences, polarization is simply an observable phenomenon, but socially we tend to think of polarization in negative terms. "When we argue, we just get polarized," we admit to our shrinks, our friends, or ourselves. Some of us pay a hundred dollars an hour to worry about something that's as good as it is bad!

Picture a couple standing on a seesaw near the middle. Their balance is uncertain, as all relationships are, but they are touching. As something comes between them, they back away from each other slowly, deliberately, matching step for step until they are standing at the ends, behind the handlebars. (After many years of relating, couples often develop the ability to leap back in astonishingly precise synchronization, reaching the ends in one or two jumps.) But isn't this "better" than a relationship in which one person or the other is always up and the other down? Given the polarized positions, the couple is still balanced and, sometimes slowly, sometimes precipitously, they can return to their former positions at the middle. The balance is threatened when the couple moves away from the middle, but the ability to polarize can assure the continuation of the relationship. ∎

MAGNETIC

I FEEL DRAWN to this word, as if pulled by a force so great I am not able even to comprehend it. I cannot resist its attraction. And yet I feel as though I have a choice. How to approach it? From the south, as I normally approach all words?

But wait. The attraction must be mutual. This word was drawn by me as well. But the attraction must not be based on the alignment of electrons, for no matter what vantage point I adopt, the same end of me is attracted to the word. Apparently it doesn't matter from which direction I approach this word. Opposites attract, and I am not opposed to this word. Obviously we are unlike each other. Likes don't like each other, and I like it. ∎

A FORCE OF ATTRACTION
EXISTING BETWEEN OPPO-
SITE POLES & REPULSION
BETWEEN LIKE POLES. (IT
WORKS WITH PEOPLE, TOO.)

magnetic

A STATE OF CONSTANT DIPOLA-
RITY; A NORTH POLE CANNOT
BE ISOLATED FROM A SOUTH
POLE ANY MORE THAN YANG
CAN BE ISOLATED FROM YIN.

ELECTRICITY

A smell of burning fills the startled air—
The Electrician is no longer there!

NEWDIGATE POEM
Hilaire Belloc

ELECTRICITY AND MAGNETISM are the yin and yang of electromagnetism. Both are based on polarized electric charges, positive and negative, that elementary particles of matter possess. Like charges repel each other, while unlike charges attract. Originally the word "electricity" referred to what we now know as static electricity—the force that causes two objects to attract each other when friction between them causes or allows charged electrons to hop from object One to object Two. But that's still a little hard to comprehend.

Stick your finger into an open socket. That's the only way to really understand electricity. It feels as if your arm were pure energy and no longer a

THE CURRENT YIN AND YANG
OF ELECTRICITY ARE THE DI-
RECT AND ALTERNATING VA-
RIETIES. DC'S CIRCUIT MOVES
IN ONLY 1 DIRECTION, WHILE
AC'S REVERSES FREQUENTLY.

A STATE OF ENERGY EXISTING
IN ALL ATOMS THAT IS CREA-
TED BY THE ATTRACTION BE-
TWEEN THE POSITIVE CHARGE
OF A PROTON AND THE NEGA-
TIVE CHARGE OF AN ELECTRON

part of your body. Soon (something like one one-thousandth of a second later), some part of your mind understands that it wouldn't be too much longer until none of you was part of your body, and you would cease to exist. Thus enlightened, you remove your finger from the socket.

Benjamin Franklin, not having any empty sockets handy, sought enlightenment with a kite, a key and a jar. The "discovery" of electricity came to him in a flash. Even though we currently generate our own electricity, it's still probably fair to think of it as trapped lightning.

On second thought, don't stick your finger into an open socket. Sooner or later, we all become pure energy. There's no sense in rushing it. Instead, take note that on page 39 is one of the rare instances of lightning striking twice in the same place. ∎

GRAVITY

T HIS IS NO time for levity. This is a grave subject (as are we all). It's time to get down to some serious etymology. We must dig down to the roots.

First of all, gravity and gravitation are different. Gravitation is the attracting force existing between *any* two particles of matter. Gravity is the attraction between the earth and any other hunk of matter. Since we and our languages developed here on earth, we see the heavens as being "up." So whereas relationships between things in space may seem more lateral, we are definitely *down* here, and anything coming toward us from the sky is definitely coming *down*—that's gravity.

The root of "gravity" in modern English is the

IS THE
SOUL
OF WT.

gravity

IS THE FORCE WITH
WHICH ONE ENTITY
ATTRACTS ANOTHER

word "grave." The two most common usages of the word "grave" are: 1. "a place of burial," and 2. "having weight or importance." In the first case, the word "grave" evolved from the Old English *grafen,* meaning "to dig." In the second instance it came from the Latin *gravis,* which means "heavy" or "important." It doesn't seem like any coincidence to me that a downward direction is central to both meanings.

In any case, if it weren't for gravity we wouldn't know which way is up. Without gravity to pull things "down," there would be no such concept as up *or* down. This is an excellent example of the yin / yang principle that nothing exists except in relation to its opposite.

In conclusion, I'll be brief. The absence or opposite of gravity is weightlessness. Therefore, gravity is the soul of wt. ■

WHAT
GOES
up
MUST
COME
DOWN

U p / D n

"I find," said 'e,

"things very much as 'ow I've always found,

For mostly they goes up and down

or else goes round and round."

ROUNDABOUTS AND SWINGS
Patrick Chalmers

THE POPULAR PHRASE this ambigram demonstrates captures the spirit of Newton's third law of motion—for every action there is an equal and opposite reaction—and the essence of yin and yang as well. It is most readily demonstrated by the force of gravity. Even the most towering home runs and foul balls eventually make it back to earth. But the idea can appropriately be extended to the fame of celebrities, hemlines, personal moods and a myriad of situations beyond the jurisdiction of the laws of physics.

It's tough to escape the music of yin and yang. Even the seemingly capricious vicissitudes of in-

M. C. Escher, WATERFALL, lithograph, 1961

dividual minds and societal trends dance to that tune. It could very well be that the laws of physics are encoded in the molecules of all our DNA, or that throughout our emergence from the world of physics into the realm of biology, and our continued presence within both, we have assimilated those principles into our individual and collective subconsciouses and, hence, behaviors. Fact is, we need balance.

What drives this tendency is obviously more than gravity. Our decisions are based on our perceptions of our surroundings. While "what" is going up, since nothing can happen in isolation, conditions are changing, often as a result of "what" 's ascent. One good example might be the stock market.

As the Dow Jones Industrial Average rises, people feel good about investing. They perceive the positive momentum of the Dow, are encouraged that it will continue to rise, and so buy. As a result, stocks increase in value and the Dow does continue to rise. This continues until the average is so high that investors, evaluating that condition, begin to question the strength of the momentum. Buying slows; selling begins. A new condition takes effect, and responding to it, investors sell and the Dow falls.

The ebb and flow of the stock market (which could be called "Dowism" but isn't) is directly related to the same human emotions that *do* respond to the law of gravity. A hot-air-balloon ride (I'm told) is exciting as it begins and exhilarating as the balloon soars over the countryside. But if the balloon were to rise beyond its passengers' expectations, nervousness would set in. That might have to do with unintentional lateral motion at first, if indeed there were any, but whether the balloon were directly over its point of origin or a hundred miles out to sea, being subject to the law of gravity would eventually be the primary concern of the unfortunate occupants. It is this very concern that has thus far kept me out of hot-air balloons and nervous on airplanes. "Look not thou down but up!" wrote Robert Browning. I couldn't agree more with this advice, and I try to follow it. When one is down, on the ground, for instance, with the attendant sense of security, looking up affords one the pleasures of studying and enjoying the sky. When people are up in an aircraft, they mostly look down—longingly, it seems to me. ∎

WATERFALLS

WATER INTRIGUES US. We love to go to the ocean, swim in pools, take showers, relax in baths and jacuzzis. We can be transfixed by water moving from one place to another—picnics by the river and playing, as children, in streams. But of all the forms of water that attract us, no other has the compelling power of waterfalls. Why? Simply because water falls. We usually take the effects of gravity for granted. Most things simply aren't in a constant state of falling. But waterfalls, in common experience, *never* stop. Each one is a part of a never-ending cycle and thus an accessible demonstration of the infinite. As such, in a most awe-inspiring manner, waterfalls appeal to our subconscious

It was hard to imagine an upside-down waterfall, so this one is a mirror-image ambigram.

appreciation for both the force of gravity and the many cycles inherent in life. Little wonder then that the Taoists consistently refer to water as demonstrating the principles of the Tao.

Water is always yielding. It takes the path of least resistance. It seeks not the highest place, but the lowest. Avoiding confrontation, it goes around whatever gets in its way. Yet it wears down everything in its path. Water gets its way by yielding.

The Tao is also about returning, and water demonstrates this principle as well: evaporating in millions of gallons a day from the ocean, descending to earth as rain and snow, then beginning its long meandering trip, returning to the sea. A journey of a thousand miles begins with a single drop. ∎

Minimum

"The tao does nothing, and yet nothing is left undone." This important passage from Lao-tzu addresses the fundamental Taoist concept of non-action. But since we are incapable of total non-action—even in the deepest meditation our internal organs are performing their functions at a minimal level: we are breathing, pulsating, digesting and so forth—scholars have often interpreted this passage as "doing the minimum."

The concept of resistance is at odds with the Taoist approach to life. Choosing the path of *least* resistance is more in keeping with Taoist philosophy, and once again, water shows us the way. To go with the flow is to get from point A to point B

IT'S THE LEAST I CAN DO.

with a minimum of effort. Accepting itself as subject to the law of gravity, water travels accordingly, circumnavigating its obstacles and eroding them in the process. Water does nothing of its own accord, and yet everything is affected by water. By doing nothing more than obeying the law of gravity, water shapes and nourishes the entire planet.

AS THE AMBIGRAM on the previous page demonstrates by giving almost no clues as to what letters are here, doing the minimum is often sufficient. It is a happy coincidence, of course, that the word "minimum" requires so little, because in *every* ambigram I have tried to do the minimum: to perform the manipulations necessary to provide both readability and reversibility. Decisions are made on the basis of what is required to meet these ends. Nothing is added that will not aid in the achievement of these goals. Form follows function.

It is certainly true that I have tried to draw the letterforms in a beautiful fashion, but that beauty is directly related to readability. The letterforms of most Western languages were brought to their classic forms by the Romans, who instilled in them all the beauty of shape and proportion that were manifested in their architecture and sculpture. Though the alphabet has undergone a myriad of stylistic experimentation in the past two millennia, most of the letters we read throughout our lives are primarily based on those classic Roman forms. Readability is most easily achieved by providing the reader's eye with attractive and familiar letterforms. In a manner of speaking, it's back to the basics. ■

WAVELENGTH

As WATERFALLS REPRESENT water in continuous motion, waves are water in continual motion. Not content simply to watch these compelling phenomena, human beings have tried to become directly involved and have devised various craft with which to ride them—to go with the flow. As it turns out, waves are much more suitable for sports than waterfalls are.

Surfers, besides attempting to perfect their athletic skill, spend hours trying to understand every nuance of the waves they ride. One of the more predictable aspects of waves is their frequency. Their rhythmic repetitions are familiar to everyone who has ever set foot in the ocean, and to physicists, whether they've ever waxed a surfboard or not.

Wavelength

IN A SERIES OF WAVES,
THE DISTANCE (IN UNITS
OF TIME OR SPACE) FROM
TROUGH TO TROUGH OR
FROM CREST TO CREST

The word "waves" may evoke the image of a beautiful day at the beach, but water is perhaps only the most visible and tangible of the many things that come to us in waves. When energy is transferred through physical matter, a disturbance is created, and the material responds (in an equal and opposite manner) to restore its state of equilibrium. The pattern created by the stimulus and the response is wave motion. This motion takes place without any corresponding progressive movement. The individual parts of the material, as the energy disturbance passes, come to rest in their original positions. Were this not the case, a Los Angeles baseball fan, returning from a Dodger Stadium food stand, might find his empty seat and his friends three sections to the left of where he left them. Fortunately, waves don't work that way.

In visual terms, the wave pattern suggests various relationships between yin and yang and other graphic representations of physical principles. Below is a diagram of waves.

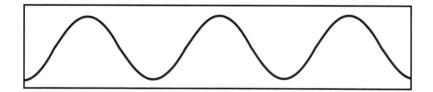

A single wave, pictured from trough to trough, looks rather similar to the curve of normal distribution.

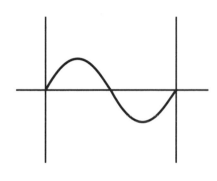

A single wavelength measured not from trough to trough or crest to crest, but from a point where the wave pattern crosses the pre-disturbance level to the next instance of that intersection, reproduces the line that separates yin and yang.

The spiral of a coil-spring toy is often used to demonstrate the action of waves, and when extended and viewed at a right angle to its cylindrical axis, the toy itself bears a striking resemblance to a series of waves.

Graphing the oscillation of a pendulum results in the same sine curve as the oscillation of particles in a wave. Simultaneous plotting of two sine curves resembles a two-dimensional representation of the double helix of DNA.

Isolating a single wavelength from the two sine curves in phase opposition yields a reasonable facsimile of the graphic symbol for infinity, while a three-dimensional model of that symbol is a looped wave pattern two wavelengths in circumference.

I could probably go on with this, but the wave is coming around again, and this time I don't want to spill my beer. ∎

Normal Distribution

THE CURVE OF normal distribution is quite familiar to statisticians, psychologists, and social and physical scientists. To those who use it on a daily basis in statistics and measurement, its accuracy in predicting patterns is doubtlessly taken for granted. Its inherent beauty, both functional and aesthetic, may often be overlooked. But its beauty can be enjoyed by anyone, anywhere.

I WAS TENSE as our plane left the runway. The trajectory was, as usual, a gradual angle at first, then more dramatic as it climbed toward cruising altitude. As the plane approached thirty-six thousand feet, its thrust and angle moderated, and my tension did the same. After a while, from the vantage point of my window seat, I watched as scattered hills rose and fell, increased in number, grew to mountains, tapered off again and ultimately disappeared into the plains. Little streams joined to form bigger ones; small rivers followed suit, eventually conspiring to create the Mississippi. Later, the process seemed to be reversed. Next to me, on the aisle, my wife caught some of the scenery. Most of the passengers missed the views, as they sat in the five seats in the middle of each row down the middle of the plane. There were, as usual, among the three hundred or so passengers, a few old people, some middle-aged folks, a large number of young adults, several teenagers and a few children. Just about everyone got up once or twice during the course of the five-hour flight. A few, mostly in the middle seats, stayed put throughout. A handful, mostly children, spent much of the time roaming the aisles, and the attendants were on their feet for all but the few minutes at either end of the flight. They were busiest around the halfway point, as they saw to the distribution of lunch. As calm as I get on an airplane, I read, slept and, after a brief period of turbulence, read again as we crossed the middle of the country.

As we neared our destination the pilot began the descent, a

HUMAN BEHAVIOR, &C.;
IN NATURE, THE ENDS
JUSTIFY THE MEANS,
SO HUMANS AMOUNT
TO A HILL OF BEIN'S.

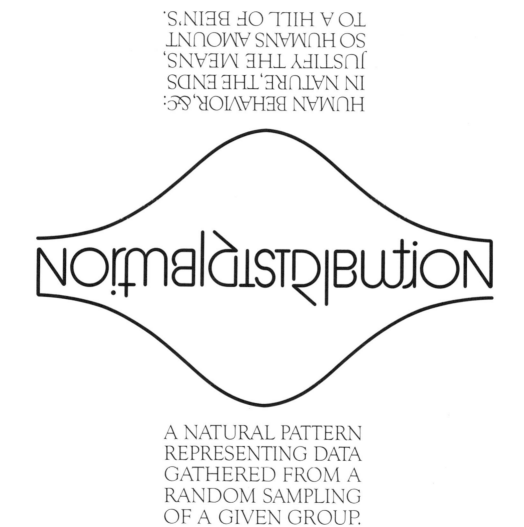

normaldistribution

A NATURAL PATTERN
REPRESENTING DATA
GATHERED FROM A
RANDOM SAMPLING
OF A GIVEN GROUP.

harbinger of the return of my anxiety. I looked out the window and tried to fend it off by concentrating on the scenery. I saw farmhouses scattered over the countryside, and here and there, a small town. One or two tiny cars ran along the two-lane country roads. Little by little the farms grew smaller, the towns larger, and both grew closer together. Near the horizon the suburbs began. As we flew over, I could see that most of the houses were small one- and two-story homes. As the city came into sight, they were larger. Soon larger industrial buildings and an occasional small office building appeared. The cars looked bigger now, and there were more of them. Passing over the center of the city, I saw it rise to its fullest height where the population reached its greatest density.

With the landing gear down and the flight attendants buckled in, we began our final approach. Despite my concentration on patterns, my anxiety increased until we had landed. The awesome power required to lift a huge airplane into flight was demonstrated again, symmetrically, with the roar of the jets and the intense braking required to slow it down.

As I was leaving the plane, still in a state of hyperawareness from my adrenaline rush at landing, I noticed that the carpet of the gangway was quite worn down in the center, less on either side, and in virtually pristine condition next to the walls.

Reflecting on the experience, I mused that there are probably precious few flights with no turbulence at all, and very few that are terrifying ordeals. It had been an average flight. But as my legs relearned earthbound equilibrium, it felt good to be in my own time zone again. Back to normal. ∎

TIME

Time present and time past
Are both perhaps present in time future,
And time future contained in time past.

FOUR QUARTETS
T.S. Eliot

WHEN I LOOKED for yin and yang within the concept of time, my first thought was, "Wait. Time exists not in a duality, but in a triad of past, present, and future." But that's merely a trio of linguistic terms. It dawned on me that the present is not my lifetime, this year, or even this week. From an awareness point of view, what happened one minute ago has more in common with what happened ten thousand years ago than it does with what might happen one minute from now. Since I now know what happened one second ago, it is clearly in the category of the past, and since, conversely, there's no telling what will happen a second from now, that moment exists in the future. The present is,

THE PRECISE MOMENT OF COMMENCE-MENT OR END OF AN EVENT.

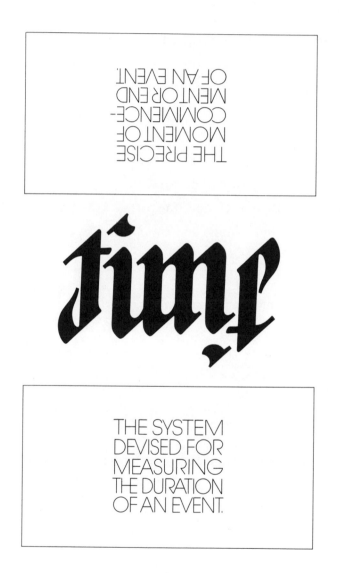

THE SYSTEM DEVISED FOR MEASURING THE DURATION OF AN EVENT.

therefore, no more than the meeting point between the past and the future—no more a distinct entity than the line where yin meets yang. Both the past and the future are infinitely long and receding lines. The present is that indefinable point where they meet.

Yet the present is where we live. The past is history, and the future is conjecture. The present is life. Looking at time from a different point of view, the past and the future exist only as concepts in our minds, and the present, fleeting as it is, is reality.

THE TWO SIDES of a knife are irrelevant to the function of the knife. The edge where they meet is where the knife's essence, its *raison d'être,* exists. The finer, the less measurable that edge is (the less it even exists at all?), the sharper the blade, and the more effective the knife. ■

Present

THE PAST AND THE FUTURE
EXIST ONLY IN OUR MINDS.

THE PRESENT IS REALITY.

THE PRESENT IS MERELY
A DIVIDING LINE BETWEEN
THE PAST AND THE FUTURE.

THE PRESENT LASTS as along as the blink of an eye. The past and the future, on the other hand, are always around and will probably last forever. The past seems to keep getting bigger with more and more of our personal and cultural histories piling up on it. The abstract future may be getting smaller, but how would we know? Certainly the future of anything we know is diminishing, but there may be an adequate supply of future for those whose lives remain beyond the limits of our imagination.

The ambigrams on these pages are intended to represent the interminable conveyor belt of time, and the individual letters and words are the ex-

periences, the "life bites" of our existence, the lines on the highway we're driving down.

Time can be thought of in purely visual terms, with the instantaneous present as the image that is currently being received on the retina. That idea seems to work in almost any situation, but let's get back in the car to extend the analogy to include the past and the future.

The future is what lies ahead along the road. The immediate and most predictable future is what's visible at any given moment. It will almost undoubtedly become part of our driving experience within a few seconds. What lies down the road beyond our scope is the more remote future. The farther away it is, the less predictable it becomes. The past, in much the same way, is what's in our rearview mirror, receding into the distance.

To fully enjoy the PAST and FUTURE ambigrams, don't use this book like a steering wheel. The rearview-mirror approach will prove more successful for the bilateral nature of these ambigrams. I hope you're not reading this while you're driving, though. Any mirror will do. ∎

SOMETIMES / NEVER

It may not be now.
It may not be soon.
It may be in the days-yet-to-come time.
But whether it's soon
or a long time from now,
there's a chance that it could happen
        sometime.

So never say "never"
and never say "always"—
there's always at least one exception.

And so if you ever
should hear in the hallways
a "never," it's always deception.

                ■

SEASONS

The byrds' popular late-sixties recording "Turn! Turn! Turn!" is an adaptation of a passage from the Book of Ecclesiastes, and thus demonstrates the timelessness of the instinctive need for balance. Citing a yin and a yang in each line, it seems quite Taoist in nature: there are no value judgments— merely appropriate times for all things.

To everything there is a season,
and a time to every purpose under heaven.
A time to be born, a time to die; a time to plant,
    a time to reap;
A time to kill, a time to heal; a time to laugh,
    a time to weep.

turn

To everything there is a season,
and a time to every purpose under heaven.
A time to build up, a time to break down; a time to dance,
    and a time to mourn;
A time to cast away stones, a time to gather stones together.

turn

To everything there is a season,
and a time to every purpose under heaven.
A time of love, a time of hate; a time of war, a time of peace;
A time you may embrace, a time to refrain from embracing.

turn

To everything there is a season,
and a time to every purpose under heaven.
A time to gain, a time to lose; a time to rend, a time to sew;
A time to love, a time to hate; a time for peace. I swear it's
　　not too late.©

CHOICE / DECIDE

THE PROCESS OF growth from infancy to adulthood, from dependence to independence, is so gradual that we are often not aware of the changes that take place until well after they have happened. Through most of that time we are told that we have to do certain things: "You have to go to school," "You have to go to bed now." Most people seem to spend the rest of their lives thinking that they "have to" do the things that they do: "I have to go to work," "I have to go to the dentist," "I have to pick up the kids."

Initially, it may seem like mere rhetoric, but YOU DON'T *HAVE* TO DO ANYTHING. Next time you find yourself on the verge of saying "I

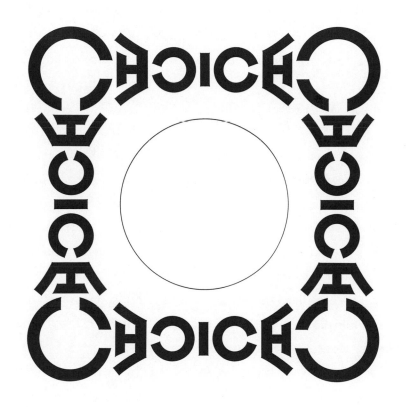

have to . . . ," try replacing it by "I choose to . . . ," "I want to . . . ," "I've decided to . . . ," or "I'm going to . . ." It's incredibly liberating! When you say "I have to," you believe it. The number of things that we "have to" do should have us feeling like slaves. Think of the frustration and damage to self-esteem that must come from thinking that you have to do everything that you do. And think of how much more powerful you'll feel when you say, "I've decided to."

AT SOME INDISTINCT point in our childhood, probably earlier than we can remember, we started doing things by choice but didn't realize it. We decided to eat our baby food because that seemed to please Mom (undoubtedly a subconscious decision). We decided to eat our vegetables so we could have dessert (more likely a conscious decision). And then one day, we *decided* to defy our parents. We realized that we didn't *have* to finish our vegetables. They could sit there on the plate for all eternity. We also learned that our decisions had consequences.

As teenagers we learn freedom. Little by little, we discover that we are independent of our parents. Often we discover it by doing what we're not "supposed" to do. How could you discover your freedom if you never exercised it? As adults, however, we soon forget what we learned. Our society seems to believe that there's something wrong with teenagers and that they'll be all right when they "grow up." And when we "grow up" we seem to believe that.

We go back to doing things that we "have to." Why do we "have to"? "Because if we don't, then . . ." That's right! There are consequences to be faced "if we don't." But there are also consequences if we do! We seem to use the word "consequence" only in a negative sense. But the word simply means "that which follows." When we *decide* to do what we "have to" do, there are consequences—usually consequences we want: we keep our jobs, we get raises, we have food to eat and a roof over our heads. Every time we do something it's because we *decide* that the consequences will be more to our liking than if we don't do it. Any way you look at it, life is a pattern of decisions.

When we tell ourselves we have to do something, it's usually in a situation where the choice between consequences is so obvious that conscious thought is not required. But that does not mean that we *have to* do it. "Have to" means that you have no choice. And you *always* have a choice. There's a story about Jack Benny, avowed tightwad, in which he was accosted by a holdup man. "Your money or your life!" the crook demanded. When

Jack didn't respond, the man grew impatient: "Hurry up, will ya?" to which Benny replied, "I'm thinking, I'm thinking!"

Reminding yourself that you do things by choice gives you the sense that you are in control of your life. You realize that you have had a choice all along. You are where you are because of choices that you have made. You didn't *have* to go to Vietnam. You could have applied for conscientious objector status. You could have gone to Canada or to jail. Or crossed your fingers and hoped that you'd get a high number in the lottery (even no decision is a decision). You chose the option you were the most comfortable with. You are responsible for your own life.

At any given moment, you could choose either to kill yourself or to continue to live. Realizing that you have control over this, the ultimate in choices, may make all the other choices seem comparatively trivial, almost easy. I can quit this job and find another one, or maybe even not get another one. That is my choice. Having made the choice myself, I am happy to live with the results of it. Or make another choice to change things again. I can leave this relationship any time I choose. Did you see *Five Easy Pieces?* You just get on the truck, and you're gone. Or you stay by choice.

HAVING A CHOICE is the same as having freedom. Many people *choose* not to exercise their freedom. They forget that they have choices. Maybe they never consciously realized it.

The idea of consequences, "those things that follow," presumes that there is a sequence of events. Some events precede; others follow. Time, then, is a major factor in the freedom of choice.

If you *always* have a choice, at any given moment in time you have a decision to make. Fortunately, most of our actions fall into that category called "The Choice Is So Obvious That I Don't Have to Think About It." Seldom while we're walking downstairs do we decide to keep walking downstairs. Nevertheless, some hidden recess of our subconscious is deciding to keep walking down the stairs. Occasionally, of course, we decide to turn around and go back up.

SINCE TIME AND EVENTS keep moving, as we've often heard, not making a decision is making a decision. Opting for the status quo (which, loosely translated from the Latin, means "standing as or where you are") is choosing to stand still and allow time and events to flow around us. Since it is technically impossible to stand still in time, we are simply "going with the flow." We should recognize that status as reflecting a decision—and much of the time, a sensible one. It is also usually the easiest decision we can make. For better or worse, our lives, and history at large, are governed for the most part by inertia. That's why it's so hard to change ourselves and our lives and our societies.

IF WE ARE making decisions at every moment of our lives, life is therefore a constant pattern of choices and decisions. Each decision brings new choices. We are always free to choose, and, paradoxically, we are never free of the need to choose. If we were able to free ourselves from the obligation of choosing, we would surrender our choice to our surroundings and give up our freedom of control.

> Every room has several doors,
> several eithers, several ors.
> Every door has several outcomes.
> Some are sure;
> with others, doubt comes.

When we make a decision, we can seldom be sure what the consequences will be. Thus life is a constant exercise in insecurity. This is probably the reason why most people are happier feeling that they have to do things rather than being conscious of the fact that they are choosing their actions. They may complain about their jobs and their spouses, but they feel secure in these relationships. Are freedom and security mutually exclusive, a major yin and yang in life? Many times we hear of the trade-off between freedom and security, particularly as it pertains to civil rights. But how secure can one feel giving up control over one's life not knowing what other events and other people's decisions are to come and what effects they might have?

Perhaps that, too, is cause for insecurity. But if one maintains the awareness that he is *choosing* inertia, *choosing* to go with the flow, with the knowledge that he can at any time change his mind and get out of the flow or swim upstream, one can remain very secure. Security comes only with the awareness that one has a choice. ■

THE CHARACTERISTIC
OF MATTER WHEREBY
AN ENTITY IN MOTION
CONTINUES TO MOVE
UNLESS ACTED UPON
BY AN OUTSIDE FORCE.

INERTIA

THE CHARACTERISTIC
OF MATTER WHEREBY
A STATIONARY ENTITY
REMAINS STATIONARY
UNLESS ACTED UPON
BY AN OUTSIDE FORCE.

INERTIA

For thousands of years it was assumed that rest was the natural state of matter. Apparently overlooking friction, among other things, Aristotle and others thought that moving objects would eventually run out of steam and return to their "natural" behavior—resting.

Isaac Newton's first law of motion upset that apple cart: "Every body continues in its state of rest, or of uniform motion in a right line, unless it is compelled to change that state by forces impressed upon it." The name given to this phenomenon is "inertia." Inertia, it could be said, is the characteristic of matter that says nothing happens to it unless something happens to it. The entire notion of inertia may itself seem inert, but there's good reason that this ringing endorsement of the status quo should be Newton's first law. Its logic was basic enough that his subsequent laws and theories, and those of others as well, could be based on something that for a few hundred years was virtually unquestionable.

Then Einstein's relativity theory challenged Newton's laws. We now know that everything in the universe is in motion, outward bound from Big Bang. Things at rest are at rest only relative to other things, which are probably resting nearby. It's like falling asleep on a train: you may be at rest, but it's still not all that restful. A geostatic satellite, on the other hand, would appear to be at rest to the geo standing under it, but all the while it's whizzing through space at hundreds of miles per hour. Like everything else, motion is relative—it depends on your point of view. ■

MOMENTUM

"Today is the first day of the rest of your life."
This statement implies that we have choices and
are in control of our destinies. While this is certainly
true, it overlooks the power of momentum. We are
the sum total of our hereditary and environmental
pasts. With the possible exceptions of God and Big
Bang, nothing has ever started from nowhere.
Everything owes its existence to something else. A
number of something elses all interacting with each
other. Everything has momentum.

The present may be the doorway to the future,
but everything coming through that door comes
from the past. Today most people live in the same
place, relate to the same people, speak the same

EQUALS MASS TIMES VELOCITY.

momentum

THE QUANTITY
OF MOVEMENT.

language and operate from the same set of norms, values and standards that they did yesterday. You can steer a car in any of a great number of directions, but the change in direction is both limited and gradual. Each change in degree is based on and is in relation to the previous degree. This need not be discouraging, however. After all, it is much easier to turn the wheels of a moving car than a parked one.

EARLY IN THE history of literary criticism, Socrates said that a story should have a beginning, a middle and an end. This is the opposite of the "slice of life" approach, in which a mere segment is treated, possibly leaving the reader wondering what may have preceded and what might have followed. This wondering is undoubtedly a result of the understanding that nothing exists in isolation—everything takes place in an infinite web of cause and effect.

Much to the frustration of many moralists, science has shown that even the beginning and end of the life of a human being cannot be pinned down precisely. A fetus is preceded by a blastocyst, a single layer of cells arranged around an empty cavity, and the blastocyst in turn is preceded by the single-celled zygote. The zygote was preceded by and made from the union of a sperm and an egg that in turn were produced by preceding human beings. At death, if there is a soul, it continues on in some way, and the body begins a new process toward some other form of energy.

In human behavior some might say that the ends justify the means, but this is a short-sighted vision. There are no ends. Each result is merely a factor in some other process. Everything exists in a state of momentum. ∎

CHAIN REACTION

For want of a nail, the shoe was lost;
for want of a shoe, the horse was lost;
for want of a horse, the soldier was lost;
for want of a soldier, the battle was lost;
for want of the victory, the kingdom was lost.

SINCE NO EVENT takes place in isolation, there are no ends but only means. Each and every occurrence is merely a link in an infinite chain. Perhaps the blacksmith, while he was shoeing the soldier's horse, was distracted by a gastrointestinal problem caused by something he had eaten the night before and therefore simply did a shoddy job.

At any given moment, there is an infinite number of identifiable chains of events operating simultaneously. Surely any hypercompulsive, omniscient scientist with infinite patience could trace any series backward in time, ultimately reaching back to Big Bang. While Big Bang itself was

probably caused by another series of events, *that* idea is currently beyond our knowledge.

In addition, each chain is intersected by other chains. Not only is no single event isolated from all others, but no single chain of events can course through time unaffected by other chains.

The meat the blacksmith ate had begun to spoil due to a series of biological events. This was not noticed by the cook due to a series of sociological events affecting his family. He had been arguing with his wife over something her mother had said to him. Her statement had triggered a chain of psychological associations that led him to think about his own mother instead of the state of the meat.

Naturally, the loss of the battle had its effect on all subsequent history, including the apparently insignificant fact that you are currently reading this book. But then the want of a nail seemed insignificant, too. ∎

ENERGY

Few of us can fully comprehend the idea that $E = mc^2$, much less use it in conversation. That aside, "energy" is a dynamic word whose different common meanings are used fairly equally in our culture. An energetic person can perform a great deal of work. We use our energy resources to effect change in our lives: to light and heat our homes and to move ourselves from one place to another. No matter what the situation, nothing is accomplished without the transfer of energy.

One of the most significant aspects of energy, particulary since Einstein established its relationship to mass, is that it cannot be created or de-

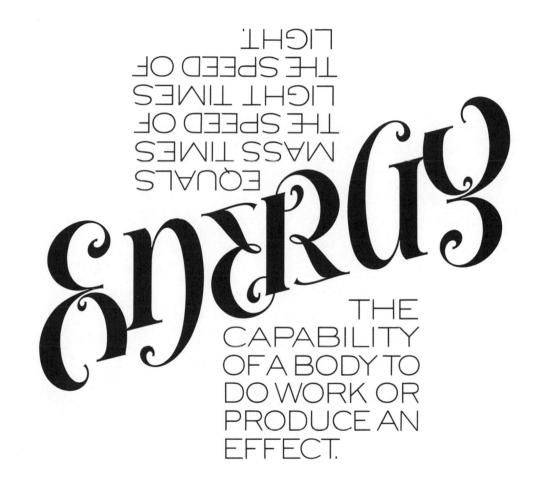

ENERGY

EQUALS MASS TIMES THE SPEED OF LIGHT TIMES THE SPEED OF LIGHT

THE CAPABILITY OF A BODY TO DO WORK OR PRODUCE AN EFFECT.

stroyed. The amount of energy present at Big Bang (which must have been a lot, given what's come of it) still exists in its various forms throughout the universe. These include electricity, heat, light, sound, chemical energy, and mass, which are all interchangeable. It is by changing from one form to another that energy gets things done.

My lava lamp represents a chain reaction of these forms and changes. The power company may transform mass, in the form of fossil fuels (which once were living organisms deriving their energies from the heat and light of the sun and the consumption of other organisms), to heat and then electricity. By plugging the lava lamp in and turning the switch from off (yin) to on (yang), the electrical energy is converted to the heat and light of the light bulb. The red goopy stuff (to use the precise scientific name) in the bottom of the conical vessel is heated, and as its density becomes less than that of the oil it lives in, it rises. The light adds to the visual appeal of the undulating goop and helps to stimulate my brain cells. I then have more energy to apply to whatever task is on my desk. But I'm not sure that this last transfer of energy follows the mathematical formulas that apply to other transformations.

A PENDULUM SWINGS to and fro, shuttling back and forth from east to west. In the west, pendulums are perceived to go, "tick, tock," but in the East they might go, "yin, yang, yin, yang. . . ." The ebb and flow of the pendulum is symbolic of many harmonic, complementary relationships. The pendulum can also function as a model for a more subtle yin and yang relationship: the inverse ratio that exists between two common forms of energy: potential energy and kinetic energy.

Potential energy, as its name implies, is energy that is not currently active but exists due to the position of the body in question. A boulder sitting in the middle of a flat plain has little likelihood of going anywhere and therefore has little potential energy. But the same boulder, perched at the edge of a cliff, patiently waiting for one or two more grains of sand to be eroded away before it plummets into the gorge below, has great potential energy.

Kinetic energy is energy that an object has due to its motion and is in proportion to its mass and velocity. Once the boulder falls, it has plenty of kinetic energy.

In its lateral path, the pendulum possesses and exerts both forms of energy. At the extreme ends of its arc, it comes to a complete, if imperceptible, stop. At that point, the pendulum has no kinetic energy but has attained its maximum potential energy. Instantly, as that potential begins to be realized, its potential energy starts to decrease, but it does not instantly disappear. Until the pendulum reaches its lowest point, in the center of the arc, its position renders it still subject to the force of gravity, and thus it maintains a degree of potential energy. Throughout the course of the pendulum's descent to its lowest point its speed increases, and so, proportionally, does its kinetic energy. At its lowest point, the pendulum has no kinetic energy; its position alone would get it nowhere. But since its velocity will begin to decrease as it passes its nadir, it is, at that moment, going as fast as it will go in the course of its arcing path. Therefore, having fallen to its lowest level, the pendulum possesses its maximum kinetic energy.

In a symmetrically similar manner, the pendulum's kinetic energy decreases and its potential energy increases as it climbs to the opposite high point. There, once again, its kinetic energy will momentarily cease to exist, while its potential energy enjoys a brief moment of maximum power.

In a thermal rather than a strictly mechanical system, the goop in the lava lamp goes through similar changes. The heat it takes on while at rest at the bottom indirectly gives it a kind of kinetic energy, which elevates it to the top of the vessel. There it rests in a state of potential energy again while it cools and its density increases. It then succumbs to the force of gravity and falls to the bottom. There the goop begins the process again, ever changing; falling as yin falls, rising as yang rises. ■

RELATIVITY

There was a young lady named Bright,

Whose speed was far faster than light;

She set out one day

In a relative way,

And returned home the previous night.

(PUNCH, December 19, 1923)
Arthur H.R. Buller

IF YOU ARE at Rome, live in the Roman style," wrote St. Ambrose in the fourth century A.D.; "if you are elsewhere, live as they live elsewhere." This point of view may have been remarkable sixteen centuries ago, which might explain why it has been kept around, albeit in a simpler form, for all these years. A more likely sentiment, increasing relative to the distance from Rome, might have been, "If you are at Rome keep thine own counsel, for the Romans are an ignorant, barbaric people." Throughout human history the people of one culture have generally distrusted and disapproved of the values and prac-

THE STATE OF BEING IN WHICH ONE ENTITY IS INTERDEPENDENT WITH, AND CAN BE UNDERSTOOD ONLY IN REFERENCE TO, ANOTHER

RELATIVITY

EINSTEIN'S THEORY THAT ALL MOTION IS RELATIVE, ENERGY AND MASS ARE INTERCHANGEABLE, AND SPACE & TIME ARE NOT ABSOLUTE

tices of other cultures. Cultures have tended to see the world the way the blind men saw the elephant. It wasn't until the relatively recent past that anthropology began to convince us that values should not be expected to remain the same from one society to the next. The fact that we have not yet learned that lesson is, however, not the point here.

HISTORY RECORDS ANY number of examples of simultaneous discoveries and inventions. This is not too surprising because people are often working within the same matrix of ideas and data. But sometimes currently accepted knowledge leads to similar developments in different fields. This may have been the case at around the dawning of the twentieth century, when there was an unusal confluence of revolutionary ideas. The proliferation of these new concepts has shaken the human tendency to believe in absolute truths—from right and wrong to space and time.

The philosophy of relativism deals with the difference in ethics in different places and times. These became more familiar and accessible as Marconi's radio and the Wright brothers' airplane heralded the beginning of intercontinental communication and a quickly shrinking world. Sigmund Freud introduced the unconscious, an alternate self, which could be blamed for un-acceptable actions as though it were someone else, thus relieving the individual of responsibility. And one of the most far-reaching ideas was Einstein's theory of relativity, which suggested that space and time are cousins and that mass and energy are twins. We may *all* be relatives of one sort or another, descended from a common biological ancestor. The ideas that have been born and nurtured over the past hundred years have doubtlessly had much to do with the uncertainty of the world we live in.

Nietzsche, in 1882, declared the death of God, and indeed, religion has enjoyed better times than the twentieth century. A minister once described religion to me as what people need "to make sense out of the senselessness of their lives." For many people, organized religion has been replaced in that role by a fatalistic materialism, zealous patriotism, or other chauvinisms. But the response has not been a unilateral abandonment of religion. Indeed the response has been predictably polarized, or balanced. Based on my minister's definition, one might think that the apparent senselessness of the past several decades would have been great for religion, and in a way that has been the case. A return to the absolute values of religion can be seen in the recent rise of fundamentalism around the world, and many of the philosophies of  are at least as retro-gressive.

Witness the interest in not only the older Eastern philosophies but more primitive, Earth-based ideas as well.

That time is not an absolute has been amply demonstrated by recent history. The breathtaking pace of events, technological developments, communications and travel seems to have left most people with a sort of cultural jet lag, and our mainstream religions seem to be the luggage lost in flight. Unable to move slowly enough to please the conservatives and purists, and unwilling to change as quickly as the progressives would like and world events seem to dictate, the religions that thrived through the nineteenth century have failed to meet the needs of their constituents at both ends of the spectrum. The absolutes that had been basic dogma have changed too much for one group and not enough for the other.

This is not to say that things would have been better without religion. Indeed, that may be, according to the minister's definition, an impossible state. But our technologies have changed at the speed of light relative to our religious institutions, and so, for many, the extremes have become the means to the same end.

Nothing lasts forever. Perhaps gods do, but the religions that worship each god will not, so the names of the gods will change, at least. Change is constant, and things change relative to what has been. Each action is in reaction to a previous action. Nothing can be defined except in terms of something else. Everything is relative. Everything exists in a state of relativity. ■

M. C. Escher, RELATIVITY, lithograph, 1953

ACTION/RE-ACTION

IT IS INTERESTING to find that the laws of physics often seem to apply to human behavior as well. Following what must originally have been an instinct for fairness, ancient codes of morality called for "an eye for an eye, and a tooth for a tooth." A crime was seen as an unsettling of the natural balances in life, and justice was an attempt by human beings to restore those balances by a punishment that fit the crime—an equal and opposite reaction. Most primitive societies accepted this approach as right and proper. Later, the principles of Christianity and other modern moralities introduced the idea of forgiveness—"turning the other cheek." While this seems, on the face of it, to be an advance in human development, one should not overlook

TO EVERY

ACTION

SIR ISAAC
NEWTON

THERE IS
ALWAYS
OPPOSED
AN EQUAL

RE-

AN EQUAL
OPPOSED
ALWAYS
THERE IS

ACTION

SIR ISAAC
NEWTON

TO EVERY

the fact that at the same time, religions that had abandoned the Earth Mother and other nature-oriented gods and goddesses were beginning to predominate, as they do today. As this more modern religious thought accompanied the development of Western civilization, which in time gained predominance in the world, man began to consider not only his new religious principles superior to those of more primitive societies, but also man as separate from and superior to nature itself. The technologies that Western cultures developed have supported this idea and helped to fulfill the Biblical directive for man to "dominate the earth." We now realize that, taken to their logical extremes, the practices associated with this attitude would destroy the conditions upon which mankind's existence depends. Nature would eventually exact its form of appropriate retribution—the extinction of mankind. The wrongs would then be punished, the balance restored. An eye for an eye.

This is not to blame the Judeo-Christian tradition entirely for our present environmental problems. Nor is it to say that, in order to live more naturally and responsibly, we must go back to the "eye for an eye" approach to justice. The idea of forgiveness is not necessarily at odds with the natural law of action and reaction.

Some scholars believe that Jesus' teachings were influenced by the principles of Hinduism and Buddhism. These religions, which developed in India in the several centuries before the birth of Christ, share the concept of karma, literally "doing," which is linked to the idea of reincarnation. The sum of one's actions in each lifetime is carried on into the next life, the status of which is determined by the quality of the soul's karma. If a person performs evil acts, even if they go unpunished in his current lifetime, his entire next life will be affected by the negative energy of that karma. So a judge or jury of one's peers is not necessary in order to bring about an equal and opposite reaction.

We need not believe in the Buddhist or Hindu doctrine of reincarnation, however, in order to make use of the idea of karma. Jesus taught that one's reward would come in the "afterlife," a subtle shift from one's "next life," and that God, not man, would be the judge of a person's actions. We may also believe that one's karma takes its toll upon the evildoer internally, within the same lifetime, and that the wrong done has a greater deleterious effect on the doer than it does on the one to whom it is done. No matter how we look at it, what goes around, comes around. ∎

PERFECTION

Faultily faultless, icily regular, splendidly null,
Dead perfection, no more.

"MAUD"
Alfred, Lord Tennyson

ICONOGRAPHICALLY SPEAKING, THE circle has always been used to represent perfection. It is both infinite and complete. This is undoubtedly a response and an homage to the inherent cycles that surround us. These cycles can be described in systems of symbols using mathematics, which is "capable of a stern perfection," as Bertrand Russell put it, and mathematics may be about the only direct experience with perfection that we can have. But math itself is not a real thing. It is a language of theory, a way of discussing the ideal. By its very definition, perfection is not attainable. Our sensitivities and powers of perception tell us that nothing is perfect. How appropriate, then, that our mathematical symbol

for nothing is a circle. Zero, while still something we can't really experience, is absolute. What else is? Only infinity, symbolically represented by another circuit.

All the same, perfection is a nice idea to have around as a carrot hanging at the end of our intellectual stick. The theoretical existence of perfection gives us something to shoot for, a windmill to be tilted at. We can improve ourselves and our efforts indefinitely. "The indefatigable pursuit of an unattainable perfection . . . is what alone gives a meaning to our life on this unavailing star," wrote Logan Pearsall Smith. That statement reminds me of my minister's definition of religion. And indeed, one of the more familiar symbolic uses of the circle is found in Christian decorative arts, where it represents God.

MINERAL CRYSTALS, CURRENTLY enjoying a resurgence in popularity by way of pop philosophy, are among the most discernible examples of perfection in nature. In their various structures, classified according to the types of symmetry they exhibit, crystals adhere to obvious mathematical rules. Our fascination with them is understandable. They invite us in, saying, "Look close. There *is* order. Things *do* make sense." They are a hint—nature's way

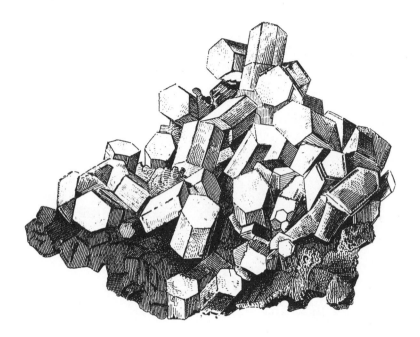

of telling us that our mathematical and scientific systems are on the right track.

In many ways, crystals are like us. No two are exactly alike; each is beautiful in its own way. We can relate to them on an emotional level because, like us, each has its flaws. Without the flaws, crystals would look like pieces of manufactured plastic. Perfection and emotion do not get along well at all.

We are never quite able to accept something on one level when it may be expanded, and our fixation with the circle as a symbol of the ideal takes on greater depth in three dimensions. The sphere is symbolic of the orb we live on and is idealized in the most mystical of all crystals, the crystal ball. The perfection of all crystals can instill a sense of calm, and the sphere may do this best of all. Concentration can produce a meditative effect, and in that state the mind of a "seer" can freely associate the shapes and patterns created by the imperfections of the crystal to the patterns of life and, some might say, the shapes of things to come.

What is always predictable, but that no clairvoyant will ever report, is death, the eternal infinite. Many religions, on the other hand, predict that death brings the attainment of perfection. One's life comes full circle. It is complete. Robert Browning wrote, "What's come to perfection perishes." But it works the other way around as well. ∎

MATHEMATICS

All things began in order,

so they shall end, and so shall they begin again;

according to the ordainer of order and mystical

mathematics of the city of heaven.

THE GARDEN OF CYRUS
Sir Thomas Browne

MATHEMATICS IS A coded language through which we can tell the gods that we are not unaware of what is going on around us. Or it may be the most self-flattering, self-aggrandizing trivia game ever invented. The English philosopher Bertrand Russell seems to have seen these two points of view. He said that mathematics "possesses not only truth, but supreme beauty—a beauty cold and austere . . . yet sublimely pure, and capable of a stern perfection such as only the greatest art can show." He also wrote that math "may be defined as the subject in which we never know what we are talking about, nor whether what we are saying is true."

WE HAVE FOUND about a zillion ways of dressing up the equal sign. You can put x on one side and $\frac{-b \pm \sqrt{b^2 - 4ac}}{2a}$ on the other. You can put E on the left and mc² on the right, or 1 on one side and 1 on the other. To really go wild, you can say that if a = b and b = c, then a = c. You can add (5 + 5 = 10), subtract (5 − 5 = 0), multiply (5 x 5 = 25) and divide (5 ÷ 5 = 1). Do with numbers what you will, it all comes down to the equal sign. The rest is symmetry.

Did human beings always know that they had the same number of digits (!) on both their left and right hands? And the same on each foot? I prefer to think that one day, shortly after the dawn of *Homo sapiens,* one individual came running back to the cave with this exciting discovery. "How obvious," we think. "E = mc²!" "How obvious," the gods think.

"THERE'S A DIVINITY that shapes our ends, rough-hew them how we will," said Hamlet. There *is* an order to the universe, and starting with the person who discovered the symmetries of the extremities, continuing through the present with formulators of theories about string, galactic bubbles, DNA, dark matter and white holes, we human beings understand some percentage of that order. Divinity, as Shakespeare wrote the word, with a lowercase d, could be interpreted as "divine-ness," not necessarily as "God." What could be more divine than the fact that Norfolk Island pines, sunflowers, lizards, and snowflakes use the same system we do?

The Taoists must have felt that human beings are part of the system. Their observations of nature guided their principles and their approach to life. But their focus was as much on the concept of opposition as on the idea of equality. The Taoists may or may not have been impressed that $5 = 5$, or even that $2 + 3 = 5$. Symbolically speaking, they focused on the fact that the numbers in question were on *opposite sides* of the equal sign. Observing the sun and moon, man and woman, night and day, they concluded that opposites are equal and in balance.

The graphic inspiration of the equal sign is not terribly well disguised: two separate elements of identical length and, every time I've ever seen it, the same thickness as well—two things that are equal. The gods may have been satisfied when we realized that things that appear to be different can actually be the same. After all, we don't seem to have progressed beyond that theme.

Every specific proof depends on that balance. Every piece of art in some way responds to the concept of repetition and variation. Things are different, yet ultimately the same. Chaos, according to the Bible, is what *preceded* creation. What follows is its opposite—order.

Is chaos, then, equal to order? Yes, in that they are the two states in which we are able to imagine the existence of all things. If they are equal, maybe one didn't simply supplant the other forever. Perhaps they alternate. Does order, then, depend on awareness?

In any case, mathematics is our security blanket. As long as we have it, we can feel that our lives make sense, rough-hew them how we may. ∎

ALGEBRA

The fact that the root of the word "algebra" means the "redintegration," or reuniting, of broken parts is intriguing when looked at through yin and yang lenses. Yin and yang is, after all, also the union of separate parts.

In trying to figure out how "algebra" came to be the name of a branch of mathematics, I first needed a definition of the word as we use it today. Algebra is the area of mathematics that focuses on relationships between numbers, using symbols to help solve equations and establish the values of unknown quantities. Let's look at an example.

$$5x + 3 = 2x + 15.$$

OF THE UNKNOWN
SUBDUE THE FEAR
WHICH SYMBOLS
MATHEMATICS IN
IS THE BRANCH OF

algebra

IS DERIVED FROM
AN ARABIAN WORD:
"AL-JEBR" — THE
REDINTEGRATION
OF BROKEN PARTS

Now, we don't know right away what the value of x is, but by first getting all the unknown (yin) entities on one side and the unknown (yang) numbers on the other, we can figure it out pretty easily.

$$5x - 2x = 15 - 3$$
$$3x = 12$$
$$x = 4$$

Plugging that back in to the original equation, we find that

$$(5 \cdot 4) + 3 = (2 \cdot 4) + 15$$
$$\text{or}$$
$$23 = 23$$

Voilà! Redintegration!

Apparently either the unknown, x, has broken away from the known values and needs to be reintegrated with them, or the broken parts fall on either side of the equal sign, and only when the value of x is established can the two sides be proven equal and thus reconciled, or "redintegrated."

Now for an unannounced, open-book quiz that was developed by an often puzzling friend, Scott Kim. This is a test. Had it been an actual alert, you would have been instructed to report back to ninth grade. Repeat. This is only a test.

Solve for x:

1. XLGEBRX

2. xray = black + white

3. 2x or not 2x. That is the question.

4. (9 + 7x/2 = (4 − 2x(6 − 2x

5. Drifxod

6. $ = mxy

7. Solve: (hint: "When in Rome . . .")

> nine
>
> sk2ng
>
> f4e
>
> se5en
>
> mo6ng
>
> s9
>
> e10it

BIG BANG

THE UNIVERSE IS probably expanding, still ex-
pending the energy of Big Bang. Its momentum
continues. But there are theories that that momentum will eventually dissipate and the universe will
then begin to retrace its steps and eventually col-
lapse, perhaps as totally and dramatically as it began. Yang followed by yin. Perhaps yin will be
followed by another yang event: Big Bang II (if
indeed our self-centered view of cosmology is cor-
rect and Big Bang was the first of its kind), ultimately followed by, well, a wavelike series of
expansions and contractions.

A black hole is thought to be a massive star
whose nuclear energy has been exhausted. Its

outward thrust of energy thus diminished, it shrinks. Succumbing to its own gravity, its mass becomes increasingly dense. The resulting gravitational pull is so great that the star not only accumulates more mass in the form of any matter within its gravitational field, it pulls light and even space toward it as well. A black hole may or may not continue in that state forever, but it seems possible that it could reach a critical mass and explode, creating what is known as a "white hole." Could Big Bang have been the beginning of only one in a series of expanding and contracting, exploding and imploding universes?

CHAPTER ONE OF Genesis reports that "the earth was without form, and void; and darkness was upon the face of the deep." Many creation myths say the same thing, with light being created in short order. It doesn't seem to me that science and the Bible are in much disagreement. If a white hole does what it's theorized to do, it would probably look a good bit like Big Bang. If Big Bang had been the product of a black hole, it would probably have had all the available light tucked inside it, though possibly in the form of mass or some other form of energy. And an explosion of that magnitude can hardly be imagined without light as a product. If *all* matter were contained in that particular black hole, there would be hardly any need for space, since space is what comes between matter, so it would have to have brought its own space with it. The void that preceded Big Bang is probably what's beyond the universe, but we may as well speculate as to what *we* were like before *we* were conceived. We can know our own lives. We can talk about Big Bang. We may even someday know the universe, but as Lao-tzu says in *The Way of Lao-tzu*, "The Tao that can be told of is not the eternal Tao." ∎

IN THE SAME way that Alan Watts saw himself as yang and the rest of the universe as yin, the earth could be yang and the rest of the universe yin. We tend to think of the rest of the universe as "other." We're here, and everything else is out there. Is this geocentric attitude arrogant? Imagine a grass seed, flung out with 21,741 others, saying to itself, "I'm special. There's nothing out there but grass seed. I'm the only one that can think."

We have no idea whether there are other sentient beings in the universe or not. Given the peculiar set of circumstances to which we owe our existence, the odds against a recurrence of those factors would seem to be enormous. On the other

"COMPELS THE SOUL TO LOOK UPWARDS AND LEADS US FROM THIS WORLD TO ANOTHER."

Astronomy

IS THE STUDY OF ALL THE BODIES OF THE UNIVERSE. IT HAS ALLOWED US TO SEE THE EARTH FROM A DIFFERENT POINT OF VIEW.

hand, given the infinite scope of the universe, what are the odds that anything could happen only once? Is the universe, like pi, a mathematically irrational system within which nothing repeats? Or is it like a fraction that does repeat but hasn't been divided out far enough to find the refrain? Our curiosity, our compulsion to understand our circumstances, appears to be as infinite as the universe.

Plato said, "Astronomy compels the soul to look upwards and leads us from this world to another." I'd put it another way. Our soul compels astronomy to look upwards and lead us from this world to another. ∎

SYZYGY

DOUGLAS R. HOFSTADTER ON JOHN LANGDON'S SYZYGY AMBIGRAM

FOR MY ENTIRE life I have been fascinated by words and names. Few words have delighted me more than "syzygy," and when I learned its astronomical meaning—a situation where three heavenly bodies (the sun, moon, and earth, for instance) chance to lie on a straight line in space—I was even more charmed. After all, there is a genuine conceptual resonance between the form and content of that word. Its content has to do with a rare astronomical lineup of three objects, and its form is characterized by three "y"s forming a rare and perfect periodic pattern, almost a syzygy of their own.

John Langdon is apparently as fascinated by this odd word and its provocative meaning as I have been, and he saw in it the potential for an elegant ambigram. Given my attraction to the periodic trio of "y"s, I find myself naturally focusing on them especially. It would be interesting to see this ambigram rendered with all three "y"s in one color, and the "s," "z," and "g" in another color—the pattern would then stand out vividly. In any case, look at the three "y"s. How much do they deviate from one another, and from more standard "y"s? On top they're all pretty similar; where they differ is below the midline.

The first of them, between the "s" and the "z," has an amusing twist underneath, reminding one of elegant curvilinear shapes like ampersands and treble clefs—and, not surprisingly, of the printed form of the lowercase letter "g." The bottom of this first "y" is, of course, the rotated *top* of such a "g."

Now let's look at the second "y." Seen in isolation, it could resemble a "z," thanks to its fishtail bottom. In the context of the ambigram, however, it is *not* alone but comes right on the heels of a very strong "z" that looks very different from it. This helps to deflect one from reading it as a "z"; in fact, a major part of the contrast between the "z" and the "y" to its right is

THE JOINING OF
TWO ENTITIES,
WITHOUT LOSS
OF IDENTITIES.

AN ALIGNMENT
OF 3 HEAVENLY
BODIES OF THE
SOLAR SYSTEM.

the "y" 's openness at the top, a feature that is necessary to define it as a "y."

Now we come to the final "y." Like the first one, it has a funny little curving tail that could distract us a bit, yet its top is so open that once again we have hardly any choice but to see a "y." To be sure, there is a little rivalry from "s," but "s"s are usually wider on the bottom than on the top, which is not the case here. This fact, combined with the open top, pretty much forces the "y" interpretation on a viewer.

Despite the considerable differences between these three "y"s, their overall similarity nonetheless strikes me. A famous research result on letter perception in reading says that the eye tends to depend on the tops of letters more than the bottoms, to provide cues to aid recognition. This fact should explain the perceived similarity of the "y"s, since their top halves are similar—it is in their lower halves that they differ greatly. The other fact that tends to bind them together is, of course, the strong and beautiful tapering lines used to render all six letters.

The overall effect is extremely pleasing to the eye, and does justice to the beautiful word—and concept—of "syzygy."

—D.R.H.

A NUMBER OF the words portrayed in this book have more than one meaning. This is appropriate, as there is more than one way to regard these words linguistically as well as visually. In the cases of INERTIA and AMBIGUITY, the meanings can even seem to be opposite, polarized at 180 degrees, just as the two visual vantage points are—and yin and yang are also. Oddest of all, perhaps, is SYZYGY. Its two meanings are different and yet apparently not opposite, but at an angle to each other. According to the *Columbia Encyclopedia,* a syzygy is the "alignment of three bodies of the solar system along a straight or nearly straight line." (A *nearly* straight line might connect the word "syzygy" with its two meanings.) The *Oxford English Dictionary* gives the Greek word for yoke, or pair, as the root of "syzygy" and then says, "conjunction and opposition of *two** heavenly bodies," and later, "the conjunction of two organisms without loss of identity" (yin and yang's favorite), and still farther along says, "a pair of connected or correlative things . . . a couple or pair of opposites." The word "three" does not appear anywhere in the list. Nowhere in the encyclopedia definition is the word "two" mentioned. What gives?

* Emphasis is mine. J.L.

One of the most vexing truths of science is that no phenomenon can be investigated without taking into account the presence of the investigator. Herein lies the disparity between the definitions: the *OED*'s definition leaves out the observer. The *Columbia* includes the earth (presumably as a vantage point) in each of its examples. But the *OED* redeems itself in its definition of "opposition," a concept mentioned by both sources in defining "syzygy." Opposition in astronomy, it says, is "the relative position of two heavenly bodies when exactly opposite to each other *as seen from the Earth's surface*."* Ironically, by adding the element of the observer's vantage point, it could be argued that syzygy has rendered itself meaningless as a concept. If it can be accepted that the earth is an arbitrary vantage point (are astronauts forbidden to use the word?), then any vantage point, at least in the solar system, should be okay. If that is the case, any three heavenly bodies can be brought into syzygy, simply by choosing the proper planet or moon to stand on.

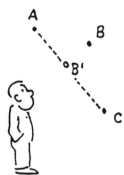

The observer in the diagram is looking at the same three stars as we are—A, B and C—but from a different place. His position is in a plane with the stars; ours is perpendicular to that plane. Whereas we do not see A, B and C as being aligned, the

*Emphasis is mine. J.L.

observer does because he sees star B as if it were in the B′ position.

The ancient Greeks apparently did not use the word "syzygy" to describe astronomic positions. In the early eighteenth century, when the word was adopted for that purpose, it must have been taken for granted that heavenly bodies could be viewed from only one vantage point—the earth. Therefore any apparent coupling, or lineup, of two bodies in space necessarily included a third—the one upon which the observer stood.

In any case, the syzygy ambigram rises to the occasion and sets the mind at ease. It satisfies both points of view. It is readable from two diametrically opposite points, and thus joins them; and as Hofstadter observes, it demonstrates a tripartite alignment. The ambigram is a syzygy, any way you look at it. ■

THEORY

*It is a capital mistake
to theorize before one has data.*

SCANDAL IN BOHEMIA
Sir Arthur Conan Doyle

ONE OF THE most interesting challenges one can encounter when indulging in wordplay is to take differing meanings of the same word and trace them back to a common root. It is a rewarding process of synthesis—a "redintegration of broken parts." The word "theory" has proven to be the most challenging of all because it brings up the question "What is truth?" and that, as we have seen, can never be answered.

The word "theory" is derived from a Greek word that means "viewing." And the divergent ways in which scientists and the general public seem to view this word are as different as black and white. Seeing words and ideas from different points

A SYSTEMATIC
EXPLANATION
FOR THAT WHICH
EXISTS, & YET ISN'T
UNDERSTOOD.

A SET OF LAWS
WHICH EXPLAIN
WHAT DOES NOT
EXIST, BUT CAN BE
UNDERSTOOD.

of view is the entire *raison d'être* of this book, of course, and "theory"'s connotations and denotations are yet another linguistic yin and yang. In the way we commonly use the word, it could be synonymous with "speculation" or "conjecture"—a hunch or a guess. For scientists, a stricter denotation applies: a theory is an idea that *can* be accepted as truth or *is* accepted as "provisionally true." The chain connecting the two meanings is forged of rather ethereal links—"Ultimate Truth," "Truth," "truth," "reality," "temporary truth," "provisional truth"—all of which might seem to be pretty similar, but it's their differences that make the chain both possible and tenuous.

A SCIENTIST BEGINS with an educated guess called a hypothesis, the validity of which is tested by experimentation. In the course of this process, certain principles may emerge that ultimately result in a system of laws that, in turn, explains the phenomena in question. That organized network of principles or set of laws is called a theory. If experimentation verifies the hypothesis, a theory is accepted as valid. For example, quantum theory and the theory of relativity are now considered to be true. They have been supported by subsequent findings and have not been disproved.

Here comes the gray area. One reason a "true" theory is not considered to be "The Truth" is the fact that it has not been tested in every place and time in the universe. Scientists hold open the possibility that ideas may be modified, supplanted or disproved by discoveries not yet made. It is this cautious allowance that leads to the more common use of the word "theory."

Whereas most people assume that there is a definite reality out there that is patiently waiting to have all of its aspects understood, scientists are more likely to accept the notion of an infinite reality, one that will always have more mysteries and engender more questions. The truths of yesteryear—the earth is flat, the earth is the center of the cosmos, and so forth—are no longer true. Each was supported in its day by observation. Making sense of our experience is what theories and "truth" are all about. Aided by what currently seems like incredible technology, we believe that our observations are a bit more sensitive these days, and the practice of science is the constant refinement of our observations. In the future we'll know more about virtually everything as technology continues to allow for more powerful, sensitive and accurate observation.

This leads to another point of confusion in the use of the word "theory." Since scientists accept the idea that there is a difference between theoretical reality and observed reality, their theories are considered to represent the ideal. This is because no study can claim to have examined *all* the aspects of any given situation. Once a *modus operandi* for a given phenomenon has been developed, it can be encoded in a formula that smooths off the rough edges of the reality. Since those rough edges actually exist, the formula represents the way things work in an ideal state—"in theory."

Scientists recognize that there is more "reality" than our technology can currently measure. But they are willing to hope and presume, for the time being, that since their theories have held up to date, any future refinements will continue to support them. This is an idealistic attitude, and scientists know that reality *may* prove to be different. We don't often think of scientists as being idealistic, but in this regard, they must be. Idealists are commonly thought to be out of touch with reality, and in common usage, an "ideal" is taken to be something that does *not* exist.

THEORIES DANCE AROUND, encircling the way things work. They describe what does not exist—an ideal—because and so that we can understand things. They define what does exist—"reality"—despite the fact that not all its aspects are or can ever be known. They describe not the way things work so much as our *understanding* of how they work.

I HAVE WHAT I used to call a theory, but I'll have to admit it's only an uneducated hunch: a mirror universe exists and we could communicate with its inhabitants through the use of ambigrams, if only we knew their XAF (extra-universal analog facsimile) number. ∎

LIMITS / INFINITY

THE STAGES OF one human being's life may be compared to the stages of development of human beings in general. The awareness of our environment increases as time goes by. Infants are probably aware, at first, only of Mother, then of other family members and home. Subsequent experience expands awareness to neighborhood and then to town. In time, more theoretical leaning brings us in touch with our country, the world and beyond, into the solar system and the universe. Eventually, in many cases, the process repeats itself in reverse, awareness diminishing as death approaches.

Throughout most of human history, people have understood and accepted limits. Primitive

humans must have spent their whole lives acquainted with only a tiny part of the world. No one in the history of the village had ever been across the river or traversed the mountain range in the distance. Life was demanding enough right there in the valley. Those with the curiosity to wonder what lay beyond the horizon or the frontier were often considered dreamers or worse, and sometimes subjected to all manner of abuse. Pushing at accepted limits has seldom been a popular pursuit. But curiosity persists as a driving human force, and as individual curiosities are followed and satisfied, eventual cultural acceptance has allowed many old limitations to fall.

As technology develops to catch up with and satisfy curiosity, cultural awareness grows. In 1609, Galileo developed the first telescope used to survey the heavens. He may also have been the inventor of the microscope, which was first used at around the same time. Any number of times since then, scientists have thought they had reached a limit—in terms of the imaginable size of the universe or the amount of material in it and, in the other direction, the smallest units of matter. In time, each has been exceeded.

The various natural systems that display themselves in mathematical terms often reveal nature's response to limits, usually

infinity

AN UNREACHABLE POINT AT THE END OF A NEVERENDING LINE THAT REPRESENTS

demonstrating the concept of approaching (but never reaching) zero as a limit. The purest and most abstract rendition of this concept would be a graphing of the equation $y = 1 / x$, resulting in a hyperbolic curve. Each leg of this curve will continue to get closer to the coordinate nearest it, as long as further values for x are determined. But like a microbe jumping from an original position halfway to a wall, then jumping halfway again, the limit of the coordinate or the wall will never be reached.

Although it is apparently growing in size, we now believe that the universe is finite. But the human mind with its apparently limitless curiosity, in an attempt to comprehend a finite universe, says, "Yeah, well, what's beyond it?" Some say the concept of infinity is hard to grasp. But in many ways, it now seems harder to comprehend limitations.

It is our understanding of the word "limits" that's a problem. What we have considered limits in the past were only milestones or boundaries. These can be passed and crossed. Ultimately, limits are what we can approach but never reach. And we can do that for an infinite amount of time. It may very well be that the finite and infinite are the same thing or are definitively braided together. Could yin exist without yang? ∎

Spirals

Is existence linear or cyclical? An argument could be made either way.

Some things, it seems, will never return. I'm counting on never having to take trigonometry again or, for that matter, repeating *any* of my adolescence. And so far we don't see dinosaurs coming around every now and then. Are they gone forever, or are they just on a slower schedule than say, Halley's comet or wide lapels? But then there are other things, like political campaigns, paying bills and doing laundry, that roll around so predictably that they may very well have their own sighting niches at Stonehenge. Not to mention sunrise, the phases of the moon, the seasons, Halley's comet and wide lapels.

A SPIRAL IS A CONTINUOUSLY CURVING LINE TRAVELING IN THREE DIMENSIONS AROUND & ALONG THE AXIS OF A CONE OR CYLINDER AT A REGULAR RATE.

A SPIRAL IS A CONTINUOUSLY CURVING LINE MOVING IN TWO DIMENSIONS AROUND A FIXED POINT AT A STEADILY DECREA-SING OR INCREASING DISTANCE.

Whenever strong support can be made for two opposing points of view, it's a pretty good bet that both are true. Thesis and antithesis are no more than polarized opposites without the unifying force of synthesis. Yin is yin, and yang is yang, even if they are across the room from each other. Yet it's hard to know what they are and what they mean until they are joined. So yes, existence is both linear and cyclical. And the synthesis of this paradox is well represented by a spiral.

Spirals, in fact, synthesize the principles—and in many ways the graphic representations of those principles—of yin and yang (repetition and variation), infinity (a mathematical figure with no inherent end), and the normal bell curve and its graphic extension, a wave pattern (rising and falling). These relationships were explored more fully in the discussion of waves (pages 58 to 62), but it seems that in fact each one synthesizes all the others.

Because the increments of time remain constant, I picture time not as a two-dimensional spiral with an ever-increasing radius, but as the sort of spiral we know in the form of a spring: always the same diameter but continuing in a linear fashion indefinitely. Looking at the spring from the end, one sees a circle. Viewing it from the side, the spring appears as a linear series of waves. Each morning, while coming at a predictable and repetitious time of day, is different from the one before and, presumably, the one to come. Every new moon, every January, appear at the same point on the circle, in a line with every one that preceded and is to come, and yet on a different point in the series of rising and falling waves of the spring.

The complexities and patterns of life can be seen in this analogy by imagining springs of a narrow diameter wrapped around the thickness of the coil of a larger spring. Each spiral is wrapped by a smaller spiral and is in turn wrapped around a larger one. A spiral representing seconds encircles the minute coil sixty times for each revolution of the minute spiral, and the minute spiral does the same to the hour spiral. And on and on. We cannot even comprehend the sizes of the largest and smallest spirals, and, very likely, there aren't any such things. No end, no end. ∎

ORGANIC

Samuel taylor coleridge wrote, "The organic form . . . shapes, as it develops, itself from within, and the fullness of its development is one and the same with the perfection of its outward form." According to *Webster's Third New International Dictionary* of 1986, something organic has "distinct members or parts whose relations and powers or properties are determined by their function in the whole." It constitutes "a whole whose parts are mutually dependent or intrinsically related" and has "a form growing out of inherent factors (as function, site) rather than convention."

HAVING THOSE PROPER-
TIES REQUIRED TO SUR-
VIVE AS A LIVING BEING

organic

HAVING A STRUCTURE
THAT IS DESIGNED TO
PERFORM A FUNCTION

THESE QUOTATIONS COULD just as well define and describe ambigrams. The letterform shapes, unlike those in conventional
typography, develop from within each specific word and are not
fully developed until the overall word, or outer form, has reached
a state of "perfection," that is, beauty and readability. The letters
are designed in such a way that their specific characteristics are
based entirely on their positions—their relationships to one
another—within a specific word. In the design of a typeface,
each letter is designed to read easily in juxtaposition with all

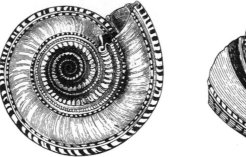

fifty-one other capital and lowercase letters. This is an open system. The design of an ambigram, on the other hand, is a closed system. The letters are designed for one specific use, in direct relationship to the letters on either side of it. That is why the O and the C in the ORGANIC ambigram are so different from the O and C in ACTION / RE-ACTION. Ironically, the G and the N in ORGANIC *are* identical to the G and N in MAGNETIC. But recent studies have shown that on occasion there may be identical snowflakes as well. ■

Change/Changes

All is flux, nothing stays still.

Heraclitus

The car has been negotiating a long curve to the left, and you've adjusted your body weight so that leaning a little to your left keeps you from crushing your ribs into the door handle on your right. Then the road changes direction. Life is like that. Any road or process in life making its way from point A to point B has to weave its way around a few obstacles and must keep readjusting to stay oriented toward its destination. If the road goes up a hill, eventually it will come down. If it curves left, it will eventually curve right. Just when you feel that you have a handle on the way things are going and can relax a little, things change.

Some may think that it's a shame
that nothing ever stays the same,
that what is good and fine today
may soon become another way.
You can't just count on things to stay
the way they were just yesterday.
Seems contradictory and strange:
The only thing that's sure is change.

Stability is considered a personal attribute. Those who shake things up are considered troublemakers. It's true that most of us, to one degree or another, resist change. We seem to want the security of knowing what's likely to come. There has probably never been a time in human history when people have not sought the advice of oracles, astrologers, soothsayers, and palm, card and tea leaf readers. And yet, without change we could know scarcely anything at all. An incessant sound, whether the interior tintinnabulations some of us carry around in our ears or the exterior drone of crickets in the summertime, eventually becomes "white noise"—a perfectly audible sound that we do not hear. I'm told that the Hawaiian language has no word for weather since it changes so little that there is no need to discuss it. I'd imagine that, confined for long enough in a bright red, empty cubicle we'd lose the sense of redness—maybe even before we went completely mad. Without points of comparison, we couldn't know anything. The senses we depend on for information about our surroundings depend themselves on contrasts: light and shadow, hot and cold, high and low pitch and volume, the yins and the yangs of our environment.

THE I CHING, or *Book of Changes,* is an ancient Chinese text of commentaries on a symbolic system that was intended to organize the complexities of life. The system was based on the dominant forces in nature, yin and yang. Chinese philosophers saw that nature was in a constant state of change as a result of the interaction of yin and yang forces, but they wanted to break that simplicity down into smaller increments in order to show greater relevance to everyday life. They surely felt there was an ebb and flow on a different scale than, say, summer and winter that could apply to the changes that occurred between Thursday and Friday.

The written form of yin was a broken (yielding) line, and of

yang an unbroken (unyielding) line:  and
Taking the two together produced yin and yang in union, but
other pairs, called digrams, were possible as well:

Yang and yang, yin and yang, yang and yin, and yin and yin.
They were arranged as a suitably polarized and balanced whole:

Continuing the process, trigrams came next, creating an octagon.
The eight trigrams were named after major natural forces and
elements, symbolically chosen for their "male" and "female"
characteristics:

heaven (☰) and earth (☷),
fire (☲) and water (☵),
wind (☴) and thunder (☳),
mountain (☶) and lake (☱).

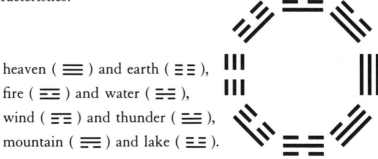

Ultimately, the full pattern was realized when the trigrams were doubled, making sixty-four hexagrams and a virtual circle. This number allowed for all possible combinations of the eight primary natural symbols and was probably seen as being about as much complexity as anyone might need or could possibly comprehend.

The *I Ching* has been used as an oracle or fortune-teller through much of its history, but like most predictors, its messages seem vague and oblique in their symbolic language. Obviously, reading that the fire brings warmth and the wind spreads the fire won't tell you whether to quit your job or not, at least not directly. The *I Ching* might say that the sun comes up out of the water and then evaporates water, in answer to the same question. What these pithy aphorisms do is remind the seeker of the major forces in life, and the relationships referred to can then be applied to the situation at hand. The interpretation is supplied by the seeker. The same thing might be accomplished by choosing at random a spiral, the infinity symbol, a normal bell curve, or yin and yang, and laying that pattern over a given situation.

The *I Ching* is particularly fascinating given the mathematical complexity derived from the simplicity of yin and yang.

Equally compelling in understanding changes are the relationships between yin and yang, with its various Western incar-
nations and the virtually limitless number of situations that life
may provide.

But change is movement. Change is growth.
Not bad or good, and yet it's both.
Our memories filled with days that passed
and brought us to today at last,
and still the moving shadows cast
ahead on what will be the past,
as time moves on and rearranges;
an infinite amount of changes.

■

BIBLIOGRAPHY

The following books were my daily companions as I wrote and were, each in its own way, important to the creation of this book.

Tao: The Watercourse Way, Alan Watts, Pantheon Books, 1975

The New Columbia Encyclopedia, Columbia University Press, 1975

The World Treasury of Physics, Astronomy, and Mathematics,
    Timothy Ferris, Ed., Little, Brown, 1991

The Shorter Oxford English Dictionary, Third Edition, Oxford University
    Press, 1979

Webster's New Collegiate Dictionary, G.&C. Merriam Co., 1961

Modern Times, Paul Johnson, Harper & Row, 1983

Ambigrammi, Douglas R. Hofstadter, Hopefulmonster Editore Firenze, 1987

Inversions, Scott Kim, W.H. Freeman, 1989

The Visual I Ching, Oliver Perrottet, Salem House, 1987